Dictation Exercises
by Elizabeth Missing Sewell

Address:
HardPress
8345 NW 66TH ST #2561
MIAMI FL 33166-2626
USA
Email: info@hardpress.net

DICTATION EXERC

By E. M. SEWELL,

Author of "Amy Herbert," "A First History of Rom
Greece for Young Persons," "History of the Early G

AND

By L. B. URBINO.

BOSTON: S. R. URBINO.

1867.

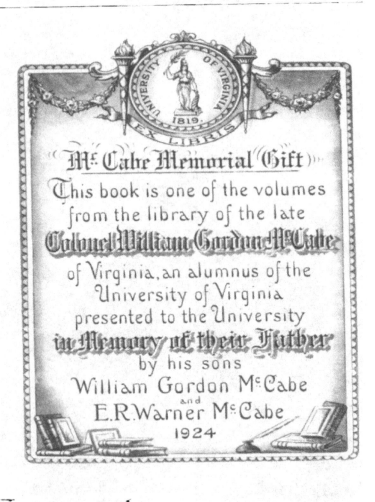

DICTATION EXERCISES.

DICTATION EXERCISES.

BY E. M. SEWELL,

Author of "Amy Herbert," "A First History of Rome," "History of Greece for Young Persons," "History of the Early Church," &c.

AND

BY L. B. URBINO.

BOSTON: S. R. URBINO.

NEW YORK:

LEYPOLDT & HOLT, 451 BROOME STREET

F. W. CHRISTERN, 863 BROADWAY.

1867.

Entered, according to Act of Congress, in the year 1865, by

S. R. URBINO,

In the Clerk's Office of the District Court of the District of Massachusetts.

CAMBRIDGE:
STEREOTYPED AND PRINTED BY JOHN WILSON AND SON.

PREFACE.

It is now generally acknowledged, that English orthography is to be taught by the eye rather than the ear.

The following exercises are founded upon this principle; yet there is no royal road to learning. Dictation Lessons may be very helpful if constantly repeated, and rules will be very useful if thoroughly understood and remembered; but to go through an exercise once, and then consider the work accomplished, is a mere waste of time.

The Dictation Exercises should first be given to the pupil to read and study till the *look* as well as the sound of the words has been well imprinted on the mind. They should then be read aloud by the teacher; and, if the whole of the exercise is considered too long for dictation, the words printed in italics should be written

[v]

down as they occur, the faults corrected, and the exercise repeated again and again, till it is perfect. This process may appear tedious; but it certainly cannot be as much ·so as the old system of column spelling.

The very few rules, which are all that can be given in aid of English spelling, ought, in like manner, to be carefully explained, and the pupil should be made to see how they apply to the words introduced into the exercise. When once they are well fixéd in the memory, a large number of the difficulties which so continually perplex young people in their first attempts at correct orthography will be found to be over-come.

Above all things, in teaching spelling, the *sight* of a word wrongly spelt should as much as possible be avoided. Exercises containing erroneous spelling are very undesirable; since, every time a word misspelt is placed before the eye, it leaves an impression which serves to confuse the child on future occasions. Parents often amuse themselves with the bad spelling of their children's letters, and it may indeed be amusing, at five or six years of age: but the consequences are very much the reverse at fifteen or sixteen, when a boy has perhaps to undergo a public examination, and finds his prospects for life injured because of his incorrect orthography; or when a girl is called upon to write a note and finds herself reduced to some petty deceit to hide her ignorance.

We often hear it said, that correct spelling is to some persons an impossibility. The writer of the following exercises begs, speaking generally, to deny this assertion. It may be a great difficulty, but — except under some peculiar and rare physical or mental condition — it is possible to all persons who will give themselves the trouble required to attain it. In instructing a child, no more mischievous assertion can be admitted than that — often so lightly made — "I never could spell." If translated into "I never would spell, because I was too indolent or too careless to make the effort," it would, in ninety-nine cases out of a hundred, be nearer the truth, and the confession consequently prove more beneficial to the character.

We resign ourselves to what we *cannot* do: we are ashamed of what we *will* not; and, with the sense of shame, there is hope that the energy may also be roused which will enable us to do better.

THE AUTHOR.

TABLE OF CONTENTS.

THIRD SERIES.

DICTATION EXERCISES.

FIRST SERIES.

WORDS PRONOUNCED EXACTLY OR NEARLY ALIKE, BUT DIFFERING IN SPELLING AND SIGNIFICATION.

EXERCISE I.

BARON S., who comes from *Ayr*, in Scotland, and is *heir* to several estates, is prouder than a Turkish *Bey*. He resides with his *aunt* in the castle amongst the *bay* trees, on the *ascent* of yonder hill. The *barren* plain at its *base* was once *bare* of houses; but the pure *air* serves as a *bait* for those who *ail* any thing, and small cottages, like *ants'* nests, have lately been built there. A large hotel, from its size called the *Ark*, was to have stood in the centre; but the baron will not *assent* to the proposal. He cannot *bear* hotels, and likens them *all* to *ale*-houses. He has, moreover, a *base* agent, who knows no more of his business than he does of a cooper's *adze* or a shoemaker's *awl*. This man *ought* to have known that building *adds* to the value of property; but, instead, he has drawn a line forming the *arc* of a circle, within which there are to be no houses. He will not have a church or a school. *Ball*-rooms, he

[6]

says, will cause persons to *bawl* and quarrel.   Shops, with *bales* of goods, will occasion disputes, and then will follow the need of giving *bail* or surety; in short, he has made the baron behave like a *bear* to the rich, and refuse to *bate* one shilling of the rents of the poor.   The baron indeed was always stingy. I once dined with him and an *anti-reformer** *at eight* o'clock.   The table was covered with a *baize* cloth; he *ate* nothing himself, and scarcely gave me *aught*. The meat provided was actually *bad*; and, though a butler with a remarkable *bass* voice stood in the *ante-room*, the baron bade me help myself.   I doubt now if e'er I shall visit him again.

EXERCISE II.

Do you see that house behind the *bole* of the *beech*-tree, close by the sandy *beach*?   I lately visited there a *beau* of the last century, who has married a *belle* of the present day.   He looked fitted for a *bier*, and as if he would soon reach the *bourn* from whence none return; whilst she with her *blue* ribbons, and gay *brooch*, and the *braid* of golden hair which *blew* about her face, seemed like a child who might have been *borne* in his arms at her *birth*. We met on the hill overlooking the bay, or *bight*, as it is sometimes called.   They were standing under the *bough* of an oak, and the gentleman being outwardly *well-bred* made me a *bow*, but the lady hid herself in the *brake*.   This caused him to *break* forth like a wild *boar*.   It was a great *bore* to me to hear

---

* *Ante* signifies *before; anti, against.*

him.   Like a *brute* as he is, he threatened, if not to *beat* her, at least to *bury* in the country.   She *bore* this well, though I saw her *bite* her lips, and gather *berry* after berry from the bushes.   At last, becoming *bold*, she told him that the *bruit* of his conduct would soon reach London ; and he, in reply, said, that, if she dared to *broach* the subject to any one, he would take a *berth* for her and for himself in the next steamer for America.   Just then an ass *brayed*, and I laughed.   The gentleman thought I was making him my *butt ; but* he was mistaken.   I left them without saying *good-bye*, hoping that they would do better *by and by*, and thinking that a man who, like myself, lives comfortably, *brews* his own *beer*, gathers honey from his own *bee-hive*, eats his own *beans* and *beet-root*, and can buy a *bole* of corn, and drink a *bowl* of punch whenever he wishes it, need not *bruise* his tender feelings by mixing himself up with divisions, which, though he may try to mend them, as a *brazier* tries to *braze* a broken vessel, must be ruptured again.   *By the by*, when the ass brays it is a sign of rain ; and that same afternoon I went to a cricket match.   The man who *bowled* best had been caught out, and I was just beginning to *bowl*, when the rain stopped the game.

EXERCISE III.

If you like, you shall have a sight of Mr. *Clarke's* letter, which you will find in that *shagreen* case. The last *clause* gives an account of a *clerk* in the *borough* of ——, which is a Cinque *Port*, and near the *site* of a Roman encampment, who means to *cite* his rector for breaking the *canon* law. The poor clergyman, who now, as the saying is, *chews* the cud of repentance, and may *sink* into his grave from sorrow, is a man of whom all who *choose*, in any fit of *chagrin*, complain without *check;* but this must be altered in another *session* of Parliament; if not, the *cords* which bind society together, and form a *caul* or network for its support, will be quite loosened. The citizens, or *cits*, as some *call* them, already hate every one who *sits* above them, as *Cain* hated Abel; and even men who cannot sign a *cheque*, but *burrow* in hovels, sitting on empty *casks*, under a smoke-dried *ceiling*, send forth complaints, harsh as false *chords* in music, and loud as the report of *cannon*, and will not hear of the *cession* of what they call their rights. For a defence against the *claws* of such persons, one must have the *casque* of an old warrior, besides the *cane* of the present day. These men, however, are *sealing* their own fate; for the better class of persons are quite against them.

EXERCISE IV.

Long *years* ago a pirate, second but to Harold the *Dane*, or the *Dey* of Algiers, summoned the *crews* of his two vessels, and bidding them give *ear* to his words, proposed to them a new *cruise*. "We have been," he said, "in many a *clime;* we have explored unknown *creeks*, and striven to *climb* inaccessible mountains. We have labored during the heat of the *day* and the *dew* of night. *Coarse cole* or cabbage, wild *currants, dough* unbaked, and even *coarser* food, varied only by the flesh of the *doe*, have been our nourishment. Our *clothes* are ragged; our shoes no longer *creak* with newness; our *fare* has been measured out as drugs are measured, by *drachms*. A *draught* of water, or perhaps a *dram* of brandy, followed by a *doze*, has been our only refreshment. Swift as the *courser*, and rapid as the fleet *deer*, no difficulties have been able to *dam* up the *current* of our success, and no scorn has been sufficient to *damn* our fame. But our *course* has not yet reached its *close*. There lives a man, by birth my *cousin*, whose trade is to *cozen*, and whose nature bids him *feign*, who would *fain dye* his hands in our blood; yet, when the deed is *done*, will surely hide his crime under the *feint* of justice. Like a vain *coquette*, who has learnt to *coquet* with her admirers, he can put on a *fair* show, and *fawn* with the light gestures of the Greek *faun*, and praise every *feat* of daring; whilst his own courage would *faint* before us, and his *feet* would *flee* from us, with the swiftness of a *flea*.

Companions and *fellows*, I give you the *cue*, and surely you will follow it. The *dun hues* of evening are gathering, the colors of sunset *dyeing* the horizon. Before the dawn arises we must *hew* down the pride of a man who is false as a forged *draft*, or the queue and the powdered wig with which our grandfathers hid their baldness. *Faint* not, nor tremble. The *feud* is ancient as the *feods* of the

days of chivalry.   To *die* will be to place our names
in the *fane* of glory; for, in *dying*, our renown will
live for ever.   The chief turned to one amongst his
followers *dear* to him above all.   "To-morrow," he
said, "is my *fête* day, and to-morrow my cousin's
fate or mine must be settled.   Dost thou dare to
follow me?"   As the *felloe* of a wheel turns rapidly,
so the eye of the pirate seemed to search for sympathy.   "I dare," was the reply.   A glad shout
burst from the assembled *corps;* but, before the
dawn broke, the *corse* of the pirate was laid in the
dust, and his followers were dispersed never to be
collected again.

Exercise V.

My boy is reading the history of *Greece;* and the
life of *Philip* of Macedon has, to use a common
phrase, given a *fillip* to his interest.   But he dislikes the constant *frays,* and the *gall* and ill-will
shown by the Greek States.   They *grate* against
his feelings like nutmeg against a *grater.*   He sees
that, in spite of the *glare* of fame, there must be
guilt in constant wars; and the *foul* stain of human
gore shocks him.   History is, however, his *forte.*
He likes to sit on the bank under the *firs,* by the
gate leading into the old *fort,* and read of the Spanish *galleons* in the time of Queen Elizabeth, and
the English ships which were in the *fore*-front of
every battle.   He knows a *great* deal about the
ancient *Gauls;* but he has *greater* pleasure in hearing about the *gage* formerly thrown down as a

summons to fight or yield. He thinks Henry the *Fourth* of France very brave ; but Henry the Third he calls a *fool*, whose *gait* was absurd, and the depth of whose folly none could *gauge*. We trust soon to take him with us to the Firth of *Forth ;* his little sister, who is as brisk as a *fly*, wishes to *flee* there at once. Just now, she brought me some *fungus*, and a kind of *fungous* substance growing on a tree, which she thought lovely. She reminds me of the wild-*fowl* which *flew* by us yesterday. I have tried to keep her still, by showing her how to *gild* a little picture of the *Guildhall*, where the *guild*, or corporation of London, meet ; but the *gilt* will not stick properly. I have heard that the *glaire*, or white of an egg, is useful in such cases. She must also put a *goar* into her frock, which is spotted with *grease*, and fasten some *galloon* to her shoes. I do not mean the lace called *galloon*, but black ribbon. In winter, when the water begins to *freeze*, and the *flue* of a chimney, and the warmth of *furs*, or of a *frieze* coat, are needed, we hope to return. Is it not strange that the same word, *frieze*, should be used for part of a building ? It is as confusing as the difference of spelling between *flies*, meaning little insects, and he *flys*, or does fly.

Exercise VI.

My friend is going to *indict Hugh* Green, the *grocer*, that *hale* man with *hair* of a dark *hue*, for *grosser* dishonesty than one should have expected. He has collected a *hoard* by cheating both in pounds and *groats ;* and has not disdained to snare a *hare,* to hunt a *hart,* to *haul* fish kept in preserves, and even to carry off a calf from a *herd* of cattle.   I *heard* the *whole* when I went to the magistrate's *hall* this morning; for I was not able *here,* in this place, to *hear* what was going on.   I was advised to *hie* thither, in order to get on a *high* bench, and see what passed with my own *eye ;* and *I* was in such haste, that I knocked down a boy trundling a *hoop.* There was a loud *whoop* when the man appeared. The crowd was thick as a *horde* of savages, and as the people trod on my *heel,* I could not help wishing for *greaves* to protect my legs.   They say that *he'll* certainly be transported.   His poor mother can do nothing but *groan,* and *grieves* till her *heart* is nearly broken; for her troubles have fallen upon her like *hail,* and this is a wound which nothing can *heal.* She is lodging now in a room which is a mere *hole,* but which is so near the south *aisle* of the church, that one can hear a *hymn* when it is sung there; and she lives like a hermit, in a *grot* or a desert *isle.* She is just now trying to *indite* a letter to one of the magistrates, who has known her son ever since he was *grown* up, and has an interest in *him.*   *I'll* go and see how she is getting on with it.

EXERCISE VII.

Mr. *Luke Leigh,* one of the Grand *Jury,* who is the son of a poor man living in the Old *Jewry,* is going to-morrow to the *levee.*   He has no *lack* of money, for he has lately come from India, where his duty was to *levy* taxes, &c.: by this employment he made a *lac* of rupees, a portion of which he would now *lief* spend in buying an estate on an *Irish lough*. The house is on the *lee* side of the lake, on a lovely *lea*. Beyond this a *lane* formerly *led* down to the water side. The garden is pretty when the trees are in *leaf;* but it has *lain* neglected for some time, and only *leeks*, and fruits for *jams*, are now planted in it. The house is *lone*, and *lacks* repair. *Jambs* are wanting to the doors, there are *leaks* in the cistern, and the *lead* is off the roof. I wonder that any one should wish even for the *loan* of it; but it is said that Mr. Leigh wishes to make a *quay*, on which coals may be landed. He is a strange person, *lax* in his principles, and sharp as a *lynx*, and keeps his plans shut up as by *lock* and *key*. Amongst the *links* which bind him to Ireland is the fact, that his *low* origin is not known there. Many fancy he is an artist, because he has tried to *limn* a little country *maid;* but I would as *lieve* give *leave* to a child to take my likeness, for he has *made* her *limbs* so awkward that the picture is a failure. *Lo!* there it is. *Look* at it.

EXERCISE VIII.

The review was very grand; the soldiers had a *martial mien;* the Field *Marshal*, as he rode through the *main* ranks, whilst his horse tossed its head and *mane*, looked proud as Darius the *Mede*, and promised them the *meed* of valor. But, though our army may be *mighty*, the enemy throng like *mites* in a *mity* cheese. The *mail* which has just come in brings news from across the *main*. It is said that every *male* of an age *meet* for war will be summoned to *meet* and fight with our troops. Our own plans are in a *maze; nought* is ready as it should be. The provisions are *naught*, especially the *meat*, and it would be *meeter* to throw them away than to keep them; but the man who *metes* them out says *nay*. This conduct is very *mean*, and there is great *need* of some reform. Soldiers, who, in defence of their country, are often *mown* down, without a *moan*, and numerous as *motes*, fill *moats* with their dead bodies, cannot *knead* their own cakes of *maize*, or provide refreshing drink like *mead*. These things must be done for them. They must have good sleep, and not a short *nap*. Their clothes must be strong, and not rotten, with the *nap* worn away. And so also for the horses; if they *neigh*, as they boldly rush to the battle-field, they should, when the battle is over, be stabled in comfortable *mews*, or at least in shelters fitted for them, and not in sacred places like the *nave* of a church, which was the stable chosen by many a *knave* in the civil wars. The government will do well to *muse* on this subject. It is nothing *new;* but those who *knew* the state of the army in the last war, fear that the evils then common may be repeated now.

Exercise IX.

The *peal* of bells which has been ringing in *our* ears for an *hour* without *pause*, as steadily as the stroke of an *oar*, will soon be *o'er ;* and, when one deep bell has *tolled*, the *pale nun* with the Grecian *nose*, and *pensile* or drooping head, which a painter would have wished to describe with the *pencil*, or with the colors of his *palette*, will be at peace. She has entered the convent to *please* herself, and has many *pleas* to bring forward for what she has done. Her brother *Paul*, the son of a *peer*, and possessing a *plum* of money, or 100,000*l.*, besides 500*l.* a year from the tolls of the new *pier*, is, as every one *knows*, worthless as a sour *plum.* He has tried to *pique* her by ill-usage ; *none* but herself can *know*, and *no* one has ever been *told*, what she has suffered. The hard *pallet* bed on which she is now to sleep, and the *pall* thrown over her at the end of the service, are but of a *piece* with his harsh words and gloom. He grasped the golden *ore* of her fortune as a beast grasps his food with his *paws.* They were a *pair* of orphans, and ought to have helped each other ; but she lived a life as dreary as on a mountain *peak.* She could not *plait* her hair as she liked, dared not indulge her *palate* by ordering *plaice*, if he had ordered whiting for dinner, and could not even *pare* a *pear* without his consent. From a kitchen *pail* to a china *plate*, all must be bought by him. He worried every one within the *pale* of his influence. A *plain* but useful servant lost her *place* for leaning over the *pales* which separate the garden from the *plain*, and talking. A footman lost his for trying without leave to *plane* some wood ; a groom for venturing to put a *pannel*, or rustic saddle, on a favorite pony; a butler for making a scratch on the *panel* of the door; and a house carpenter for injuring a *plumb*-line, left on the premises by a builder. If a jury-roll, or *panel*, could inquire into Paul's conduct, he would be declared insane.

EXERCISE X.

Always remember the difference between *rhyme* and *rhythm.** Rhyme is the effect produced upon the ear by similar sounds, such as rhyme and time. Rhythm is the accenting of syllables or words, so that they have the effect of verse. When I was a boy, my tutor, who always *pries* closely into the studies of his pupils, found that I could *read* well, but did not *reck* how careless I might be in spelling. He *rapped* me on the knuckles; but I still made a mistake between *quire*, meaning twenty-four sheets of paper, and *choir*, a band of singers; or between *quarts*, meaning several pints of beer, and *quartz*, which is a kind of mineral. I was *wrapped* up in conceit, and fancied myself *rapt* in ecstasy over poetry which I had scarcely *read*. So the tutor brought a *primer*, bound in *red*, containing a list of words, and putting on a *primmer* look than usual, and holding in his hand a stiff *reed*, told me not to *wrest* words from their *right* meaning, but to *write* them *rightly*, and not to confuse *rite*, a form 'or ceremony, with *Wright*, a workman. He showed

---

* The word rhythm is of course not inserted here on account of any similarity of sound between it and rhyme, but because its meaning is frequently misunderstood.

me the difference between *rhyme*, a sound, and *rime*, the hoar frost; *pray*, to petition, and *prey*, spoil or plunder; *pour*, to empty out, and *pore*, to look closely over; and also between *pole*, a long staff, *poll*, the head, and *poll*, to collect votes. My tutor then *prayed* me to sit down, and write from dictation. A child often *prays* to be excused a difficult lesson; but this time I did not try to *raise* my eyes, though the *rays* of the sun *poured* on my head, as I *pored* over my copybook; and the earth, being damp after *rain*, sent up a vapor like a teakettle when it begins to *reek;* whilst the noise of men who were seeking to *raze* the opposite house to the ground much disturbed me. I went through the *reign* of Henry the Eighth, and described how the king determined to *wreak* his revenge on Cardinal Wolsey, for his ambition. I received *praise* from my tutor; and was then ordered, like other boys in my class, to *write* some verses on the same subject. The distinction between rhyme and rhythm was explained to me, but I did not understand it. I had a *practice* of fidgeting; my hands were never at *rest*, and I used to *wring* the buttons off my jacket, or pull the bell-rope, so as to *ring* the bell. My tutor wished me to *practise* being quiet, and in trying to do this my attention was drawn off, and I made a sad *wreck* of the verses. The *rhymes* were correct, but the rhythm was so bad, some lines being too long and some too short, that I lost the *prize*. This *preyed* upon my mind, and made me unhappy; but I never again forgot the meaning of rhythm.

2

EXERCISE XI.

A strange story is told of Rollo and his Northmen, who, in former days, undertook to *sail* across the *seas*, and *seize* the city of Rouen, the capital of what is now called Normandy. One *sees* at once, that this was a bold determination; for neither the King of France, nor any monarch of *sane* mind, would be likely to *cede* Rouen or the country round it. The *see* of Rouen was one of the richest *sees* in France, and the land bordering on the *sea* was very fruitful. The *seed* sown there was productive; corn and *rye*, with every *root* fit for food, were abundant, and there was a good *sale* for all articles, and *room* for trade. The Normans were a *rude* people, who scoffed at the sign of the Holy *Rood* or cross. They feared no danger, cared not for *rheum* or fever, and only desired to obtain every *rood* of land possible. They used a *seal* for a signature; but the wax was not like our *sealing* wax. They did not trouble themselves to *ceil* their rooms, which in fact had no regular *ceiling*, but only a kind of *rough* roof. Some of their race, who had in other days taken the *route* through Normandy, and *seen* the lovely *scene* on the banks of the river, seem to have settled there before, and though no one *wrote* on account of their adventures, *their* children most likely had learnt them by *rote*. The beautiful *rose* of Normandy, and the wild *roes* which ran in the forest, were probably as well known to them as the *roe* of the fish which, when they went out to *row* their boats, they caught in nets, perhaps not unlike that now called a *seine*. The province was given up to Rollo ; and Charles the Simple, King of France, sent word to the Northmen that they must come and do him homage by kissing his foot. So they came ; but one of them, who was wild as a *satyr*, and cared nothing for the king, though he sat on a throne with fine robes and a worked *ruff*, gave vent to his *satire* in action, as he did not dare do so by words or a *wry* face, and taking hold of the kings's foot nearly tripped him up.

EXERCISE XII.

The *steppes* of Russia are vast in *size* and extent, though of *slight* value. They are celebrated more for the *sighs* of the exiles who have been *sent* to dwell there, than for the sweet *scent* of flowers, or the produce of the seeds which men *sow* in the ground. *So* it is that little is found which thieves would *steal*, or which it would require a sword of *steel* to defend. Time passes at a slow pace. The women *sew* their children's clothes ; the children gather berries as sour as the *sloe*, or watch the *cyg-nets* as they sail acoss the dreary lake, or the birds as they *soar* into the air ; whilst the men, the very shape of whose *skulls* shows that they are fitted for higher things, pace the *shore* with lagging *steps*, and *stare* sadly at the peasants who, in boats small as the *sculls* on an English river, attempt to cross the dark waters. It must be a *sore* trial. How many per *cent* die of *sheer* weariness, and would gladly end life even by falling over a *shear* precipice, cannot be told; for the *soul* thus exiled is *sure* to be sorrowful, and the mind, whose *sole* object is to get rid of the burden of time, must at last wear out the body. Better to *shear* a sheep, to scrub a *stair*, to practise *sleight* of hand, to *cere* threads with which to make cere-cloth, to have any employment, than thus, like the *scions* of Russian families, whose *signets* show them to be of noble birth, to have but one thought, — that of a longing for home, as deep as the longing of the Jews when they recalled the threats of each ancient *seer*, and mournfully thought of *Sion*.

Exercise XIII.

I was brought up in the country. I enjoyed the *sweet smell* of the wild *thyme*, and delighted in watching the carter driving a *team* of horses. The world then seemed to *teem* with enjoyment. Whether I had to mount a *stile*, or helped to root up *tares* from among the wheat, or to *tow* a boat along the canal, I was happy. The only trouble I had was when made to do a *sum* in arithmetic, or when scolded because I had a *tear* in my dress. The bright *sun* alone made life pleasant; and, as my father watched his *son* grow up, he must have looked forward *to* a life of happiness. But the time of change arrived; my father became rich, and we lived in *too* fashionable a *style*. I was one of a royal *suite*, and learnt to bow before a *throne*. I sat in the front *tier* of boxes at the theatre, and shed many a *tear* over some imaginary sorrow. I felt a *throe* of agony when I had an unlucky *throw* of dice at the gaming table, and when I *threw* again, hoping for better fortune, anxiety thrilled *through* my whole body. The companions amongst whom I was *thrown* began to *tease* me. They told some *tales* about me to my friends, and I was reduced to a great *strait*. I had not *two* farthings *to* buy even tin *tacks ;* and my father at last refused to advance me *two** pounds to pay the *tax*-gatherer ; and, being *too* proud *to* ask him a second time, I determined to leave to leave the country. After this I had many adventures. I sailed through the *straits* of Gibraltar ; and, making my way *straight* to China, there traded in *teas :* but, though I was *subtler* than when I was a boy, I was not so honest. The trade failed, and I followed the army as a *sutler,* and walked until I injured my great *toe.* At length I came back to London, and drove a brewer's dray, which was drawn by two huge horses, one of which had a long *tail.* The dray carried *tuns* of beer, that seemed to me to weigh several *tons.* There my troubles ended. The brewers paid me well, and with their help I have been able to maintain myself ever since.

EXERCISE XIV.

My boy knows only a country life ; he has always lived near a *wood,* and *would* not know how to find

* The words two, too, and to, are repeated on account of the mistakes often made in writing them.

his *way* through the streets of a town. I must *weigh* this consideration well before I alter my residence, for it is one of great *weight;* and I would rather *wait*, and even appear to *waste* my time, than make a change too suddenly. All *wares* and articles of dress will no doubt be cheaper in a town. This tea-*tray*, for instance, and this lace *veil*, would cost much less there, and my boy will not *wear* out so many clothes. Here, he not only grows so fast that his *waist* is too large for his jacket, but, like the *wether* and the *ewe* in the field, he is out in every kind of *weather*, and *whether* it is hot or cold he runs after the *yoke* of oxen as they drag the loaded *wain*. When he comes in to tea he is so hungry that he eats the *yolk* of six eggs, so that we pay several shillings a *week* for eggs. Once, however, his strength was on the *wane*; but now he is no longer *weak*. You are very kind in urging your wish; but I feel as changeable in my opinion as the *vane* of the weathercock, and it is in *vain* to ask me to decide. To-morrow I may be in a different *vein* of mind. I confess to *you* that I am poor; but I have lived in this *vale*, and in sight of the ancient *yew* in the churchyard, till I cannot think of leaving it without a *wail* of regret. If I wish to go any *where* it is to the sea. I once went there to show my boy the skeleton of a *whale :* he was delighted with the high *waves*, and used to wade in the water, and when we went on board a vessel he learnt to know every part, from the mast to the gun*wale ;* but *when* he came home he was so feverish that he drank a *ewer* full of water, and was quite ill for some time, and had a *wen* on his neck. You see, therefore, that if you had gained *your* point, and persuaded me to move directly, you might have had cause to repent. Prudence is, however, a strong *trait* in my character, and therefore I can only say I will *waive* my objections, if possible; and, when I have well *weighed* the matter, perhaps I may *vail* my opinion to yours.

EXERCISE XV.

Young *Abel*, who has just been sent to prison, was a *boy* of whom an ancient *augur* might at once have foretold evil, unless he would *alter* his ways. He was one of a *brood* of children wild as *Barbary* apes, who paid no reverence to church or *altar*. They not only cut down every *cypress* in the churchyard, but bawled aloud the responses in church, laughed at the clergyman's *bald* head, *bored* holes with an *auger* in the *board* on which they placed their books, scribbled over the *calendar* instead of saying their prayers, and considered it the business of every *Briton* to show that he was a native of *Britain* by drinking home-*brewed* ale whenever there was a *bridal* in the parish. Their mother was a silly woman, who was *able* to do nothing except to make *barberry* jam, and *calender* the curtains which she undertook to wash. Their father was a *seller* of wine, and had some *Cyprus* wine in his *cellar*, which he bought of our ambassador at the Ottoman *Porte*. Their uncle was a schoolmaster. His *choler* was often excited against

Abel, who did not know how to distinguish one word
from another ; but was always confounding *censer*, a
vessel in which incense is burnt, with *censor*, one
who finds fault ; or *castor*, a name for a beaver, and
also a particular kind of oil, with *caster*, meaning a
person who casts out.   I have seen him seize the boy
by the *collar*, and threaten to take *counsel* of the
magistrate as to what should be done with him ; but
it would have been more easy to *bridle* a tiger than
to keep Abel within bounds.   Any one who tried to
censure or punish him was obliged to hold a *council*
beforehand as to the best mode of doing it, or he
would be sure to escape.   One can only hope that as
a *buoy* set in the sea warns ships to keep out of the
way of danger, so the fate of this *boy* may be a warn-
ing to all others.

Exercise XVI.

In the town of Colchester there once lived a
gentleman who was not only a *councillor*, or member
of the Privy *Council*, but also a *counsellor*, or person
who gave *counsel* to his friends.   He was a *deviser*
of many new plans ; but it was often as difficult to
carry them out as it is to discover the exact *divisor*
in a sum in arithmetic.   He was also a student of
ancient *lore*, and wrote a book upon the form of the
Greek *lyre*, in which he said, that every one who had
written upon the subject before was a *liar*, and took
a *lower* view of the use of the instrument than was
right.   He had *higher* thoughts about *holy* things
than his friends imagined ; and, although he often

appeared *wholly* bent upon his own pursuits, he did much to *lessen* the difficulties of his relations; indeed, he was·kinder to them than any mere *guest* could possibly have *guessed*, and *studied* their happiness as a boy studies his *lesson*. Thus he became the *depositary* of their sorrows, and his handsome writing-case, *studded* with brass knobs, was the *depository* of many secrets, especially those of a nephew who had a *lien* or claim upon an estate, and could not make it good. He was fierce as a *lion* to his servants, *fined* them if they displeased him, and gave them to eat bread made of coarse *flour;* but their *hire* was large. His death was caused by an accident. He was always a *culler* of every pretty *flower;* and one day, as he was about to gather a wild rose of a very bright *color*, he stumbled over a *load* of bricks left by a mason who had been putting a *layer* of mortar on a wall. A cow, which had *lowed* gently only a few minutes before, seeing him *lying* on the ground, rushed upon him, like a wild beast from its *lair*, and *gored* him in the left side. The poor gentleman was taken home; but his left leg swelled to the size of a *gourd*, and looked as if it had been *dyed* purple, and soon afterwards he *died*.

EXERCISE XVII.

Peter, the *miner*, was rather a *meddler*. He one day found fault with the way in which the groom in the service of the *mayor* managed the *mare* his master *rode*, and which was an animal of great *mettle*. The groom told Peter, that he might be a judge of *metal* and salt*petre*, but that he knew no *more* about horses than a *mower* of turf.   Peter, who was standing near a *medlar* tree, struck the groom with a branch, and the mayor, thinking this a bad *precedent*, had him brought before the *president* of the society for assisting miners, who decided in favor of the *plaintiff*, and Peter was fined, and in consequence left his work.   Peter's great friend was a boy of high *principle*, to whom he *owed* money.   Peter took him to one side, and asked his help again.   In a *plaintive* voice the boy said, that, being a *minor*, it was out of his power; but he thought that if Peter became a *sailor* he would do well, as he was a good *rower*, and had *rowed* often on the river by the side of which the great London *road* passes.   Peter *sighed*, then *roared* with laughter, and said he might *profit* just as much by being a carpenter; for he knew what was meant by a *rabbet* of wood, and never confounded it with *rabbit*, an animal.   The fact was, he might as well have tried to write an *ode* as to tell whether a vessel was a good *sailer* or a bad.   He could *not* reckon how many *knots* an hour it would *sail;* and, if a *mist* had come on, he would surely have *missed* the port.   It needed the knowledge of a *prophet* to know what should be done.   At last a *pact* was made between the two.   They made a *sale* of some of their clothes, *packed* up, and set off for London.   By the time they arrived, they much needed some one who could have *soled* their shoes, or been a *sewer* of their torn clothes, which were not half as neat as those of a man who has been a *sower* of seeds in the field. But they had a *staid* look, and when they asked for employment at a shop where *stationery* was sold, it was given them. They *stayed* there willingly, and indeed have remained *stationary* up to this time.

Exercise XVIII.

The Isle of *Wight* is sometimes spelt like *white*, a color; but this is a mistake. Some think the name is derived from Guith, a Saxon word meaning division. Wight also means a person. The *tide* must have flowed between the island and the mainland, and vessels must have *tacked* about in the sea which divides it from France long before it was conquered by the Romans. Those were days when chiefs could not *wield* the sceptre alone, but met at the Druids' feasts, whilst cymbals sounded, and the natives assembled from the *tracts* of rough *weald*, thick as the *wood* through which the Indian *tracks* his *way*. The inhabitants knew nothing of the sacred *symbol* of Christianity. No bell had *rung* for a service, or *tolled* for a funeral. The *wares* then sold *were* few. The *weal* of the people depended on the *wheel* of the war-chariot. The music of the *viol*, or the amusement of a game like *whist*, by which men now seek to *wile* away time which they *wist* not *what* to do with, *were* little needed in a country *where* men had to *whet* their appetites by hunting, and yet wot not how *wet* they might be before they could get food. Ye who complain of the troubles of these *wicked* days, and think that in *past* times men *passed* through life as easily as through a *wicket-*gate, consider how you *would* like to have believed the tales *which* were told by a *witch* or a Druid. Children, you may *whine* over your sorrows, and show the *weal* made on your backs by the school-master's whip: *yea, ye* men may have *wrung* your hands in anger over the follies and the want of *tact* of those who call themselves *Whigs* and Tories, and may quarrel like our grandfathers, *whose* like-nesses are drawn in full-bottomed *wigs* and worsted *hose*, and who drank *wine* as freely as we drink *whey;* but, if you will *weigh* the difference between a heathen and a Christian, you will own that heathen joys must have been rooted up as easily as the laborer *hoes* weeds out of the ground, and found to *wither* as flowers in a *vial* without water; and, *while* this was the case, and men were *tied* to earth, *whither* could they turn for comfort?

Exercise XIX.

WORDS OFTEN CONFOUNDED.

The *attendants* of my sick friend were very dili-gent in their *attendance;* but it is said that, *except* he had been willing to *accept* the *assistance* of Mr. M., a surgeon, it would have been impossible for any one to *effect* any good. Two of the *assistants* of Mr. M. called the last day, but the servants would not *accede* to their request, that they might have *access* to the sick man's room. This was from an *excess* of zeal, and, in their *adherence* to their mas-

ter's wishes, they no doubt did *exceed* their duty.
Since my friend's *decease, divers* reports have been
spread as to the nature of his *disease,* and the physicians have given *diverse* opinions as to the remedies which should have been used. When doctors
thus *differ,* it is difficult to *defer* to any one in particular; and, though we may show them outward
deference, the fact that they do thus·*dissent* from
one another must make a *difference* in the estimation
in which they are held. There is a very *apposite*
saying as to the *opposite* opinions of medical men, —
" Who shall decide when doctors disagree ? " The
surgeon, who is a man of *decent* ability, wrote a few
weeks ago a short account of the case, to which he
has since made an *addition* of several pages. It
has already reached a second *edition.* Dr. G., who
lives at the entrance of the *alley,* near the *descent* to
the river, was once Mr. M.'s *ally ;* but now he does
not *cease* to laugh at him, and *to seize* every opportunity of making unkind allusions, and declaring
that his mind is full of *illusions,* and that he did not
understand the symptoms of my friend's illness,
which was first brought on by eating unripe *currants.*
The *adherents* to this opinion are numerous, and the
degree of credit they have obtained is great. The
current of public opinion is, I fear, against poor Mr.
M.; for a foolish *ballad* has been composed against
him, and a *decree* has been passed to prevent his
being chosen as surgeon to the hospital when the
election by *ballot* takes place. I forgot to say that
my poor friend had taken care to *insure* his life, in
order to *ensure* a provision for his children.

EXERCISE XX.

I was sitting yesterday near the *fissure* in the cliff, reading the only volume *extant* of an *eminent* writer upon the *monetary* system, when I was interrupted by the *gambols* of some ragged children, who were teasing the *fisher*, by using sticks as *missiles* with which to injure his *fibrous* net, the *fibres* of which seemed too weak to hold what he had caught.   A *monitory* word stopped them, and I then began to talk to them.   One little boy, who was eating a *radish* and some *celery*, looked ill ; but I did not discover the *extent* of his illness, till I perceived that he had a *reddish eruption* on his face, caused by having used by mistake a *liniment* intended for mother.   The *lineaments* of the child's face were sweet, and the expression *ingenuous ;* indeed, his countenance reminded me of a *statue* by an ancient *sculptor,* whose *sculpture* is well known.   I was inquiring where he lived, when a Roman-Catholic priest, with a *missal* in his hand, came up to me. He knew the boy, and told me that he belonged to a party of Irish *emigrants,* who were on their way to America, and whose *auricular* confession he was called upon to hear.   He spoke in an *oracular* way upon the subject of emigration, and told me that the *statutes* of America are such as to encourage *immigrants,* who yearly make an *irruption* into their country, and finally settle there.   So many poor let *loose* upon a spacious *tract* of country, without any person to *track* their course of life, must *affect* the whole nation, and have a bad *effect* upon society. This little boy's father, he said, was an *ingenious* man, and likely to have a good *salary ;* but there were many who would, he felt sure, never be able to *emerge* from their low condition, or *soar* to anything higher than the occupation of a *sower* of the ground ; whilst others, like stones thrown into a pond, would *immerge* deeply in evil, and *lose* the very virtues they now possessed. One old man especially, with *grizzly* hair, but strong as if made entirely of bone and *gristle*, was, he said, evidently an *impostor*, accustomed to carry on *illicit practices*, though it was difficult to *elicit* from his neighbors any information about him. He might by a specious *imposture illude* some kindly disposed persons, and even *elude* the vigilance of the police ; but there could not be the *least* hope of his real improvement. I agreed ; for a man who *practises* such arts is like one who *gambles*, he finds pleasure in evil. I said to the priest, "There must be *imminent* peril for a child in such companionship, and one is inclined to *prophesy* great evil from it." His reply was, "Yes." One must indeed fear *lest* the *prophecies* should come true ; but a good pastor, an *eminent* man, very *wary* and full of *patience*, is going with them. His presence will be a protection ; and, as his *advice* will be useful, I shall *advise* them to attend to it. Leaving a few *presents* for the poor people, especially any sick *patients*, and a *razor* for the boy's father, I returned home by the *pasture* fields, in which an old *racer*, who had long left off *gambolling*, was

feeding upon some turnips, which had been allowed·
to *rot*.   After having *wrought* so well, this seemed
but poor food ; and, *weary* though I was, I went to
its master, and offered to buy it.   He consented,
for he had been *gambling* and wanted money ; but
he amused me much by calling my *proposition*, or
offer, a *preposition*, or name for a part of speech.
He might as well have confounded *capital*, a chief
city, with the *Capitol*, or citadel of Rome.

SECOND SERIES.

RULE I.

MONOSYLLABLES, or words of one syllable, ending with a single consonant preceded by a single vowel, double the last consonant when they take an additional syllable beginning with a vowel.

Monosyllables ending with a single consonant preceded by a diphthong, or two vowels, do *not* double the consonant when they take an additional syllable beginning with a vowel. Thus, *dot* becomes *dot-ted; heat, heat-ed.*

EXERCISE I.

I *thinned* and *trimmed* the *shrubbery* yesterday, and was much *heated;* for I *toiled* all day under the *hottest,* most *broiling* sun I ever felt. But the *reapers* were still more *fagged.* One man almost *fainted,* and I saw his boy *running* to the *druggist's* shop for help. They *seated* him under a tree; and, as I was *digging* near, I went up to him. He was *sitting up,* and when I *tapped* his arm, he *looked* at me, and *rubbed* his brow as if *stunned.* Then he *moaned* and *groaned,* and said his head was *spinning* round.

I *stripped* off my coat, *wrapped* it up like a pillow, and *propped* it up with a stone, and he leaned against it. The boy came back *sobbing*. He had been *stopped* and *robbed* by a lad of *greater* strength than his own, who had *rapped* him on the head, and, being *skilled* in *drubbing*, had *beaten* him, and talked of *strapping* him to a tree. *Hearing* this I *begged* the child to go back with me; but he wished to be *waiting* on his father, and *shunned meeting* the lad: so, *bidding* him stay quiet, I *planned* a way of *catching* the fellow by *popping* upon him suddenly. I no *sooner* saw him than I *scanned* him well. He was *strutting* about, and *bragging* of his doings to another lad who had *squatted* upon the ground, and was *roaring* with laughter. As I drew *nearer*, I *slipped* behind the young *robber*, and, *pulling* a *knotted* cord over his head, *pinned* his arms. He *screamed*, but *stirring* was useless; and I *dragged* him off, and took him to a magistrate, who had him well *flogged*. The man who had been *reaping* is *getting* better.

———◆———

RULE II.

When words ending with *double l* are compounded with others, or when the termination *ness*, *less*, *ly*, or *full* is affixed, one *l* should be omitted, as *al-ready*, *al-most*, &c.

There are, however, a few words in which the two *l*'s are still retained. The greater number are embodied in the following exercise : —

EXERCISE II.

I was standing last winter near the church *belfry*, looking at the view. The *stillness* was *almost awful*. The *dulness* of the heavy grey sky foretold snow, and the *chilliness* of the air caused a *chillness* in the feet which was *fully* sufficient to produce *chilblains*. The *waterfall*, stopped in its *downfall*, was frozen; the grinding of the *millstone* was no longer heard. The *millrace* was checked in its course, and the *bulrushes* in the pond were motionless. It was a picture of *still* life which, if a *skilful* artist had been at my *elbow*, I should have desired to carry away; but, *skilless* as I was, I could but gaze *until* the *tallness* of the lengthening shadows, the *shrillness* of a railway whistle, and the sight of a man running *down-hill* to catch the evening train, warned me that I must say *farewell* to the scene, and return to *fulfil* an engagement to drink tea with a friend, and eat *allspice* cake. I felt *unwell* as I entered my own door, and *albeit* not given to fancies, and *withal* most anxious to receive my friend's *welcome*, I knew that it would be for my *welfare* to remain at home. But a *wilful* feeling came over me, and *although* my symptoms were serious, the *smallness* of my actual sufferings made me think little of what might *befall* me. I went, and the consequence was an illness which lasted *altogether* five weeks.

RULE III.

When an affix, or termination, beginning with a consonant is added to a word ending with *e*, the *e* is retained, as *pale, pale-ness; sense, sense-less.*   The only exceptions are *true, tru-ly ; awe, aw-ful ; judge, judg-ment ; abridge, abridg-ment ; whole, whol-ly ; lodge, lodg-ment ; acknowledge, acknowledg-ment ; and due, du-ly.*

EXERCISE III.

The child is a *homeless* wanderer, brought up in *careless* and *shameful* habits, and it is *truly* sad to see how *rudely* she behaves.   In my judgment her case is *wholly hopeless ;* but it is *awful* to be brought to such an *acknowledgment.*   It is *true* that praise, when justly *due,* is an *inducement* and *encouragement* to further *amendment ;* but *wholesome* warnings, when *duly* given, are often needful.   I send you an *abridgment* of the child's story, merely to show the *enticements* and the *spiteful* efforts which have been used to draw her from her present *lodgment* under my roof.

———◆———

RULE IV.

When an affix, or termination, beginning with a vowel is added to a word ending with *e*, the *e* should be omitted, as *cure, cur-able ;*

love, lov-ing. Singe, singe-ing, and swinge, swinge-ing, are exceptions to the rule, as they would otherwise be confounded with *singing* and *swinging*.

If, however, the *e* is preceded by *c* or *g* soft, and the termination added is *able*, the *e* must be retained, as *peace, peace-able ; charge, charge-able*.

So also when verbs end in *ie, ye, oe*, and *ee*, and the termination *ing* is added, the *e* is retained, as *hie, hie-ing ; agree, agree-ing*.

EXERCISE IV.

The poor man's disease is *incurable*, and as he is a *loving* father, and a *peaceable* and *agreeable* neighbor, all are *agreeing* that it is *desirable* to help him. One *roguish* fellow with a *stony* heart is an exception. He says that the man was *changeable ;* that one day he took to *dyeing*, and another to *hoeing*, and that now he must be *chargeable* upon the parish. The *arrival* of the nurse is a great comfort. She will be very *serviceable*, if only in keeping the children from *singeing* their clothes. Their condition in their little *lodgings* was before deplorable. Their father was ·*grieving* for them, and, in *pursuance* of his wish to save expense, he was proposing the most *inconceivable* and *unimaginable* plans. The alteration now is *noticeable* and *observable*. The children have become *manageable* and *guidable ;* they no longer sit *poring* over the fire, but are *striving* to make their father's food *palatable*, and whilst *eyeing* the nurse and *seeing* what she is doing, they are *vieing* with each other to be useful.

———◆———

RULE V.

The plural of English nouns is usually formed by the addition of *s* or *es*, although there are many exceptions to the rule. This plural termination is often confounded with '*s*, which is the sign of the genitive or possessive case. Thus *doctors*, the plural of *doctor*, is not distinguished from *doctor's*, belonging to a *doctor*. The following exercise is intended to exemplify the distinction.

It should be observed that when the plural ends in *s*, as it usually does, the genitive case is marked by the addition of the apostrophe (') only; thus, we say *the two sons' fortunes*, not *the two son's fortune*. The same omission is, on account of the sound, sometimes made when the singular ends in *s*. We say *for righteousness' sake*, not *for righteousness's sake*, but this is more a question of choice and ear than of rule.

The possessive pronouns *hers, ours, yours, theirs*, are often written *her's, our's, your's*, &c.; but this is a mistake.

EXERCISE V.

The *farmer's horses* have been sent to bring the two London *doctors*. The groom said that the old *horse's* foot was hurt; but the *horses'* appearance when they set off was splendid. No doubt the *physicians* will expect large *fees*, and, in a case like this, all *fathers* would give them willingly; but your *father's* income is small, and his *expenses* are great. *Charles's* education, and little *George's*, with that of the two *Harrys*, their *cousins*, must cost *sums* of money, and *Thomas's claims* and *yours* will soon need attention. The *cousins' expenses* will indeed soon be at an end; but *James's* illness is a serious matter. An *invalid's tastes* are always expensive; I know this from my two *brothers' whims* during their long *illnesses*. They were constantly wanting new *books*. One day they delighted in *travels, accounts* of wonderful *adventures, calculations* of the *heights* of *mountains*, the *torrent's* force or the *valley's* depth; but the next the *gipsy's* thefts or the *robber's* daring alone interested them. *Tales* of *robbers* were, I must own, their chief pleasure. *Walter's* favorite story in the *Arabian Nights' Entertainment* was one about *thieves*, and *William's* was the same, and I think *James's* taste is like *theirs;* but he can read little now. Your *mother's fears* are awakened; for her trust in *Mr. Green's* judgment has been less ever since she went to Wilson, the *druggist's* shop, and learnt what his *prescriptions* were. I was at the bank that same

day, and heard two *boys* talking to the. *banker's*
clerk, and telling him that *James's symptoms* were
worse, and that your mother's wish was to have
further advice.   Few *mothers* would have borne
anxiety with such faith as *hers*, and few *fathers'*
tempers would have stood such behavior as *Mr.*
Green's.   *Mothers' alarms* are indeed often un-
founded, and *parents'* anxiety will often be unrea-
sonable; but *theirs* is only too *well* grounded, and I
await the new *doctor's* decision in trembling sus-
pense.   The *lady's maid* will, I hope, come and tell
it me soon; but *ladies' maids* like to take their own
time in all things.

——◆——

RULE VI.

As a general rule *y* at the end of a word is
changed into *i* when another syllable is added;
thus, *holy* becomes *holiest; pity, pitiful,* &c.
But when *y* is part of a diphthong, as it is in
all words ending in *ay, ey, oy,* or *uy,* or when
the termination *ing* is added, it is not changed;
attorney becomes *attorneys; buy, buyer; carry,*
carrying.   Proper names when made plural
also retain the *y,* as the *Henrys,* the *Fannys.*

EXERCISE VI.

What *beauties* those *babies* are who are riding on
the *donkeys;* and the children picking *daisies* are

quite as pretty, if not prettier. Just now they were looking at some *monkeys*, whose *propensities* to steal, and whose many *whimsies*, amused them much. Now they are going *blackberrying*, as *blackberries* are plentiful. I should prefer *ponies* for riding, donkeys have such *fancies ;* but a child's *joys* are very simple ; *puppies*, *lilies*, and *poppies*, at that age give as much pleasure as *rubies*, and bread is eaten as *happily* as *jellies*, *kidneys*, or *turkeys*. Children know nothing of *villanies* and *atrocities*, *incendiaries* or *turnkeys*. *Academies* and *seminaries* are their only dread ; at least, if I may judge from the two little *Marys*, my cousins, the elder of whom says that, when she *marries*, her *studies* will cease, as *ladies* have only to take *journeys* for *enjoyment*, or go to pleasant *parties*. A *busier* or *giddier* child than the elder Mary never lived. She is also the *rosiest* and *merriest* of all the children belonging to the *families* near us. The younger Mary is *greedier* than the elder. *Delays* in the *supplies* of *dainties* make her impatient. She is, moreover, *lazier* and *sillier*, besides being the *clumsiest* and *ugliest* child I ever saw. But she has good *abilities*. She can act *comedies*, and understands somewhat about picture *galleries ;* and, though she *replies hastily* to a question, she is generally right, and seldom needs to make *apologies*. Her *eccentricities* are great : *volleys* of abuse would only make her *readier* to put *annoyances* in the way of her teachers, and, in fact, do them all the *injuries* in her power ; and as it is *easier*, so it is *happier*, for her to be governed by kindness.

RULE VII.

In writing words which commence with the prefix *dis* or *mis*, mistakes are sometimes made with regard to the omission or insertion of an *s*. In all such cases it is needful to consider whether the word to which *dis* or *mis* is prefixed begins with *s*. If so the *s* must be retained. Thus we write *dis-satisfy*, *mis-state*, &c.

Exercise VII.

Mr. Jones, the surgeon, is *disappointed* and *dissatisfied*. He has been trying to prove that *dissection* is always necessary in cases of death from unknown *disease*. But Mr. Smith is no *dissembler*, and says that it would be *dishonest dissimulation* to conceal his *dissent* from this opinion. Mr. Jones takes pains to *disseminate* his own views, and does not *distinguish* between public and private duty. No one can *dissuade* him from his course. A *dissyllable* will express my opinion of him; he is a donkey, who not only *misspends* his time and his money, but by *mischievous misstatements* and *mistakes* causes the conduct of others to be *misconstrued*, and *misdemeanors* to be attributed to them.

RULE VIII.

Monosyllables and words accented on the last syllable, ending with a single consonant preceded by a single vowel, double the final consonant when they take an additional syllable beginning with a vowel. Thus *permit* becomes *permit-ted;* but *expect, expect-ed.* When the accent is on the first syllable, the final consonant is not doubled. Thus, we write *prefer-ence, defer-ence,* not *prefer-rence* or *defer-rence.*

Exceptions to this rule are to be found in words ending with *l,* which usually double the consonant, and also in *worship-ped, worshipping, bias-sed,* and *unbias-sed.**

EXERCISE VIII.

The task of making known to Mr. —— that he was *ballotted* for yesterday, but not *elected,* was *allotted* to me. I found him in the *wainscoted* parlor, *apparelled* in a handsome dressing-gown. Tears *bedimmed* his face as he was *compelled* to own that the *preference* thus shown for another man, though much to be *regretted,* was not *unexpected.* I *proffered* my help: but my attempt at *counselling* was useless; he *preferred* to wait until he had *conferred*

* In most American books these exceptions are not admitted.

with the uncle who has *abetted* his conduct.   By *accepting* what I *offered,* he thought he might be *committing* himself to an unwise course of action. I *demurred* to this idea, thinking that he would not be *benefited* by the *conference;* for his relations have always *libelled* him, and *murmured* at him for *contemning* their opinion, and their *murmurings* are not likely to be *lessened* now.   Unfortunately his *repelling* manners have from the *beginning* shown that he was *bigoted* to his own views.   His father has *annulled* the permission given him to join Mr. ———, the great traveller, or, at least, he has *trammelled* it with *limitations* which have the effect of *repealing* it; and I *omitted* to tell him that he will no longer be *permitted* to see the cousin whom lately he has *visited* constantly, and of whom, to use a common phrase, he is a decided *worshipper.*   He *fidgeted* indeed so much, and, keeping his eyes *riveted* on the *carpeted* floor, seemed so overcome by the *distressing* news I brought, that I could not venture to say much.   His cousin will, however, be no loss, for she *coquetted* with another person whilst pretending to like him, and, though he *pocketed* the affront, he cannot have *forgotten* it; and it is my *unbiassed* opinion, that under any circumstances the *worshipping* could not long have continued, but that *quarrelling* would soon have begun. If *duelling* were in fashion, the man who has *rivalled* him would have but a bad chance.

DOUBLE—SOUNDING CONSONANTS.

In many of the words introduced into the following exercise, the middle consonant, though it is not really doubled, sounds as though it were, in consequence of the accent falling upon it. Words which *do* double the consonant are mixed with them for the sake of practice.

EXERCISE IX.

That woman has been convicted of *felony*, and is to be banished to one of the *colonies*. She has lived with the *baroness* ever since her *marriage*, and has now *robbed* her of a rare *agate*, and some *coral*. She has also *damaged* a *damask* table-cloth, by washing it in *alum*, and has stolen a *calico chair-cover*, and some lace from a *bodice*. She gained *credit* at shops, and bought *elegant* dresses with *money* which had been put into a desk in a *closet*, in the time of the Irish *famine*. She was *civil* in manner, and very *clever ;* but she drank. *claret* out of the *cellaret*, and gave it to a *bevy* of friends. In fact, she has not an *atom* of *honor* or *honesty* in her. Her mistress used sometimes to treat her with *rigor*, and at other times to *cherish* her. One day she *allowed* her to *copy* the *pattern* of one of her dresses. The baron was known to *cavil* at this: but the *baroness*, who, amongst several *blemishes* in her character, is as quick as a *comet* in her resolutions, did not pause to *balance* his opinion against hers ;

and when the baron had left the *apartment,* and was *seeking* the hare in its *covert,* she chose to *commit* the *body* of her dress to her maid, who, while *busy* in making another for herself, stole the lace. The baroness is very *learned.* She studies *botany* and *conic* sections, and has *written* sketches of *bigots* and *cynics,* and the natural history of the *camel.* She was trying to find out whether a *dragon* was a real *animal,* when a *fellow* belonging to a public-house in the *city,* called the *Civet Cat,* came to tell her that, as he was in the garden *collecting fagots,* and looking for fruit in which there were no *maggots,* he had seen her maid put the lace in a box, and *bury* it. The *intelligence* came upon the baroness like the report of a *cannon,* or the storms of a *deluge.* The police were sent for, and all the woman's thefts were *discovered.* I do not *pity* or *commiserate* either party. The baroness tried to *harrow* up my *feelings* by an *account* of all she had undergone in the *dismissal* of her *favorite* servant ; but the fact is, that she gave for wages a *pittance,* not enough for a girl living in a *hovel,* so that she might *naturally* have expected to be *cheated.*

Exercise X.

DOUBLE-SOUNDING CONSONANTS — *continued.*

My *memory* lingers with pleasure on the *many* delights of the old *Manor* Farm. *Minutes* spent *there* were *happier* than hours spent elsewhere. As a child, I used to *grovel* continually amidst heaps of *gravel*-dust, and *frolic* undisturbed by the *menaces* of my nurse, who at home was a *model* of strictness, and always *threatened* to break my *noddle*, as she *called* my head, if I was too *merry*. But her power did not extend beyond the *limits* of home. She could not *harass* me at the Manor, where the *caresses* which my aunt used to *lavish* upon me made up for the want of the *luxuries* which *money* can purchase. At first, I am *afraid* I caused much *misery* and *havoc* amongst my aunt's pets at my *annual* visits. I was in the *habit* of *teasing* her *rabbits*, and used to hang a piece of *linen* or *woolen* over the *linnet's* cage, to make it think that night was drawing on ; but I had no *malice* in my nature, and when I learned by *hazard* that I gave pain, it so *saddened* me, that it was no *merit* in me to leave off. Sometimes I used to watch the *lizards* basking in the sunshine on the *level* green bank. Sometimes I would *hover* about the beehives, trying to discover how the bees made *honey*. At other times, I helped the cook heat the *oven*, and squeeze *lemons*, or searched for *melons* in the hotbeds ; or rode in the *wagons* going to the corn-fields. The only *sorrow* I knew was, when called in-doors to practise the *gamut*, to do sums in *addition*, or read about the *feudal* system, and the *ceremony* of doing *homage*. My aunt liked *novels*, and when I went into the parlor for *dessert*, often told me the *stories* from which she could educe a good *moral ;* and I read to myself tales of *brigands* in *forests* and *deserts*, and of pirate *frigates*, and castles where knights drank wine out of *flagons*, and stood firm as *granite* rocks when called upon to fight their *enemies*. But even the *promise* of *medals* and prizes, to be given according to my *deserts,* did not overcome my dislike to the book with the *vermilion-colored* binding, which contained the History of England.

Exercise XI.

DOUBLE-SOUNDING CONSONANTS — *continued.*

My aunt wished me to become a capital *scholar*, but she could not afford a *salary* for a tutor. Though very *modest*, she had herself much natural *talent*, and loved *study;* and the *tenor* of her conversation, especially when her *travels* were her *topic*, was always useful. Her *manners* had the *polish* of a *palace*, and her *language* was *rapid* and *eloquent*. The *brilliancy* of her conversation used to *rivet* the *attention* of the person whom she *addressed*, whether he *happened* to be a *prelate*, a *privy-councillor*, a *provost*, a *sheriff*, or a *parish clerk*. Her *relish* for wit was great, and she was wont to *revel* in sharp sayings. I can see her now, dressed in her *satin* gown, and feeding two *pelicans*, which she kept in a little *pavilion* near the *river*. They were once in *peril* from me; for, when my aunt was out of the way, I shot at them with some *arrows* taken from a little *quiver* which had been given me; but *happily* I did not touch them. She would have been like a *rabid* dog, if she had known what *ravage* I was trying to *commit;* but *generally* she was as gentle as a *seraph* and as wise as a member of the *senate*. It was a *terrible* day which was to *sever* me from her, and to *separate* us for *ever*. I have *never* been able to *unravel* the *horrible* mystery *connected* with it, nor have circumstances *developed* the reason for her consenting to send me from her. I know only that in the *zenith* of my enjoyment, when my *spirits* were in full *vigor*, a man ugly as a *wizard*, and accompanied by his *valet*, and a woman dressed as a *widow*, were seen to *traverse* the hall. My aunt and I were eating *salad* for luncheon, without a *shadow* of fear of what was *coming*. The maid was in the *cellar*, striving by the help of a *chisel* to alter the *spigot* of the beer-cask. The stranger entered the room. " If you are the *tenant* of this house," he said, whilst the *venom* of *malice* and *arrogance* showed itself in his face, " this boy must come with me." —— " First make your claim *valid*," replied my aunt, and she caught hold of the *valance* of the chair-cover for *support*. I turned *suddenly*, as on a *pivot*, and struck the stranger, who *immediately* clutched me as with the *talons* of a beast. My aunt *fainted*, but was restored by a *tonic*. The stranger unfastened a ring *attached* to a chain by a *swivel*. " This is my token," he said ; " after a long *travail*, I have found you." —— " My boy, for a *million* of *shekels* I would not part with you," said my aunt ; " but your father is going to the *tropics*, and you also must go." The stranger *motioned* me to *follow*. I longed to be a *rebel*, but I dared not. My aunt kissed me fondly ; and then, mounting a *spavined* pony, I set off home. Soon after, I found myself

4

in the *cabin* of a *vessel*, and we *sailed* for *Jamaica*, where I have since *lived*, and where my life has been as *vapid* as *tepid* water, and as *sterile* of joy or beauty as that of a *sluggard* or a *sloven :* but the *recollection* of my juvenile *happiness* is always *cheering ;* and upon this my thoughts are ever *dwelling*, and must still *continue* to dwell.

EXERCISE XII.

IRREGULAR SOUNDS OF THE DIPHTHONGS EI AND IE.

(In this and several other exercises, words which are not examples, but have similar sounds, are introduced for practice.)

My *dear Friend*, — I *believe* I am right in saying, that the police have *received* information of the *height* and appearance of the *thief*, and that he will soon be *seized*. It will be a *grief* to many, who I know will *vie* with each other to *shield* him from disgrace ; and my *niece*, especially, has *besieged* me with petitions for mercy, and thinks she shall *achieve* her object. But she *neither* knows me, nor *perceives* the *heinousness* of the criminal's conduct. *Either* she or I must give way ; and as, on principle, I cannot *lie*, and dare not *yield*, I will not *feign* compliance. The man has acted like a *fiend* to his wife, and *deceived* every one. IIis guilt is clear : the marks of his footsteps in the *field*, and near the *weir*, where the bag was discovered, the *piece* of his neck-tie, and the lost *sieve* and *pie-dish* found in his kitchen, form *weighty* evidence against him. The wrong he has done cannot be *retrieved.* *Thieving* is so natural to him, that to overlook this offence would be only giving him a *brief reprieve* from punishment; for it would *speedily* be repeated, and greater *mischief* would follow. My *chief* regret is for his wife, in whose *veins* flows some kindred blood, and who, I fear, will not *deign* to ask for aid; but would, as people say, as *lieve* starve in a *foreign* land as beg for help. With the *view* of saving her from such a fate, I purpose obtaining for her a small yearly pension, in *lieu* of the occasional *relief* she has hitherto had. Will you *weigh* this suggestion? for I fear that, *pierced* as she is with sorrow, and inclined to *inveigh* with *fierce* anger against the *neighbor* who *inveigled* her husband to *irretrievable* ruin, her natural pride and *conceit* may lead her to adopt a stern *mien*, and thus to *freeze* the hearts of those who would *fain* help her. Heigho! There are many *grievances* in this sad world. But I must *leave* off. I hear the *neighing* of my horse, and must *seize* the *reins*, and mount, as he is restless. I fear I may have tried your *patience*, and perhaps troubled your *conscience.* Comfort yourself with the *belief* that you will hear no more of me for a long time. I sail from England to-morrow, in a vessel *freighted* with goods for *Friesland.* Before my return, I hope to try the northern *sleighs*, and the *weight* of an *eider-down* quilt, and to look upon the *frieze* of the *Parthenon.* I *hie* to these distant lands, with a heart in which, as you will *easily con-*

ceive, care *reigns;* but I find consolation in the thought, that, if I *die,* my *heirs* will enjoy what has brought no pleasure to me.

Adieu, yours, &c.

EXERCISE XIII.

SIMILAR SOUNDS OF ER, OR, OUR, AND RE.*

My dear Friend, — The person you name is as unfit to be a *tutor* as I am to wear a *mitre.* You must seek for one less greedy of *lucre,* and of higher *calibre.* Ugly as an *ogre* and *sombre* as a *sepulchre,* his *languor* and *torpor* give him the look of a *spectre. Nitre* and *saltpetre* are less harsh in *flavour* than are his words. He has not an *acre,* yet he longs for *splendour,* and talks with *fervour* of the *lustre* of an *ancestor* who prevented a *murder* at the *massacre* of St. Bartholomew. He is a *censor* of poetry, and thinks he understands *metre* perfectly. He delights in a private *theatre,* in which he is sometimes allowed to be an *actor.* If you were to *reconnoitre,* you would now and then hear him making a *clamour,* and see him crowned with a *sceptre* and holding a *sabre,* striving, with *meagre* attempts and assumed *valour,* to pass *muster* amongst good *performers;* whilst in reality he is in a great *fluster,* and trembles in every *fibre,* and is as *inferior* to others as *pewter* to *silver,* or the *colour* of *ochre* to the *glitter* of gold. He is a *suitor* for the hand of my *daughter;* but she

* In modern spelling, *or* is often used instead of *our;* thus we may write flavor, honor, labor.

has a *horror* of him, and his *ardour* only makes her *labour* to treat him with *rigour*. *Rumour* says, that she once looked upon him with *favour ;* but this is an *error*. She stood *sponsor* with him for a little *sister,* when I thought him *fitter* for the office than I do now ; and he was the *donor* of the table moved on *castors* which stands in her room : but he is at present in very ill *odour*. I think myself she will marry either our *rector*, who is an excellent *pastor*, or else *Major* G——, the *brother* of the great *sculptor*, and the cousin of the young *sailor* of the same name, whom we saw on board the frigate which was such a capital *sailer*. *Candour* compels me to say, that I should *consider* the *former* marriage the greater *honour*. Major G—— is the *inheritor* of a good fortune, which accumulated whilst he was a *minor :* but the *tenor* of his conduct is not good ; and he has lost his *vigour*, and *suffers* much from *tumours*. *Vapour* baths have been tried, but they only lull him into a *deeper stupor ;* and his servant is in constant *terror*, lest in one of these fits he should die. I hope, therefore, that the *rector* may be the *victor*.

EXERCISE XIV.

B AND N SILENT.

My dear Friend, —— We are greatly *indebted* to your brother for his account of a visit paid to the *catacombs* last *autumn*. If, like him, I could *climb* mountains without fear of injury to my *limbs*, I should rejoice to visit distant *climes*, and wander amidst the *solemn* ruins of the past.   But the *numb-ness* of age warns me, that I shall soon be *condemned* to pay the *debt* of nature, and that, instead of visiting the *tombs* of others, I must prepare to enter my own.   Much should I enjoy, however, to taste even a few *crumbs* of the knowledge he has *doubtless* acquired; to discuss with him some *subtle* questions as to the *hecatombs* of the ancients, and the period when the heathen oracles became *dumb;* and to learn his opinion of some *redoubted* heroes of old, whom I strongly suspect were more worthy of being *contemned* than honored.   I should also like to show him a *comb*, said to be Roman, and a piece of lava, on which there is a mark like a *thumb;* and, if I had time, I would put to him some queries as to the *columns* of Pæstum and the *jambs* of the doors at Pompeii, to say nothing of an inquiry as to the *hymns* used by the early Christians, and how much greater our knowledge of the more *subtile* fluids is than that of the ancients.   All this, however, must be left till we can sit down to a leg of *lamb* and a bottle of port, and talk at our ease.   Yours, &c.

Exercise XV.

IRREGULAR SOUNDS OF EO AND AU.

My friend was in *jeopardy* yesterday from a well-known *curmudgeon*, who, though dressed in *gorgeous* clothes, *assaulted* him with a *bludgeon*, as he was returning with his *aunt* and cousin *Laura* from a *jaunt* to see a ship-*launch*.   He was *sauntering*

along, and *laughing* with *George*, a stout *yeoman*,
the son of his old *laundress*, and his *staunch* ally,
when the man came up. *George* held a *truncheon*
in his hand; and, not being *daunted* by seeing a
stranger *haunting* my friend's steps, turned round
and *taunted* him; and he, in great *dudgeon*, threatened
to throw him into a *dungeon*. Two or three people,
who were rolling a *puncheon* of beer along the road,
took part with the *gaunt* ruffian. My friend escaped
with a blow on the head, which a *surgeon* soon
cured; and, as he afterwards made a good *luncheon*
from the remains of a *haunch* of venison, and a
pigeon pie, with cold *widgeon* and *cauliflower*, and
a *sturgeon*, which, however, was not much better
than *gudgeon*, I hoped he had not suffered much.
I hear, however, this morning, that he has an attack
of *jaundice*. He is ordered a *nauseous draught*,
and told to keep quiet; but this is difficult, as the
spirit-*gauger*, who lives on one side of him, plays
the *hautboy* all day, and a man who lives on the
other side takes *laudanum* till he is as wild as a
leopard, and sings songs all night. The end will be,
that before long a *scutcheon* will be hung over my
friend's door, to show that he is dead.

Exercise XVI.

G, H, AND K SILENT, AND GH HARD AND SILENT.

(The Conquest of the rebel city of —— .)

The *fight* was over, and *night* drew *nigh*. The
ensigns of a *foreign* power — the *signs* of the *sover-*

eignty of a new *reign* — were no longer seen by the *burghers* floating from the *high* towers of the city. *Poignant* was the regret of the rebel leaders as they saw the *cognizance* of the *seigniors* whom they had chosen *consigned* to degradation. Some, *aghast* at the treaty with the enemy, though they did not dare openly to *impugn* it, declared privately, that it was too *tough* to swallow; and quoted *apophthegms* to prove that, *although* seemingly well *weighed*, and *fraught* with good to a few, it would prove a *thorough slough* of ruin to many. Others boldly *arraigned* the plan of the *campaign*, and *besought* their *neighbors* speedily to execute *condign* punishment upon the generals. But the cool *phlegm* of the *benign knight* by whose means peace had been *wrought*, and who scarcely *deigned* to reply, even when his deeds were most bitterly *inveighed* against, soon brought the greater number to a more *resigned* mind. *Eight knaves*, however, like *gnarling* dogs, dared openly to *malign* him: one, especially, who was a *shipwright*, said that he had *brought* a *blight* upon their hopes; that they would never kneel to the conqueror; and that a *feigned flight* for a time would have been less shameful than giving up their *rights* after such a *slight* resistance. But *although* they thus *oppugned* him, and *gnashed* their teeth in rage, and hissed and *coughed* at him, they could do *nought* besides; and the peasantry — *delighted* with the *bright* prospect of being restored to their *plough*, whilst their wives *kneaded* their bread, and having felt the *weight* of the *ghastly* and *ghostly* horrors of war — no longer *sighed* for glory. Even if they were ruled with a *tight* hand, they *thought* it better than carrying *knapsacks*, whilst their crops were *naught*, and their children, to whom not even a handful of *dough* could be *assigned*, were suffering the *gnawing* pangs of hunger. When the *soughing* of the evening breeze was heard through the *knotted* branches of the *gnarled* oak which stood on the *knoll* above the town, they collected round it, and, recalling their past *fright*, and the *mighty* power of their adversaries, owned that *aught* but submission would have been folly. If they had *sought* excuses for themselves, they might have complained of the leaders, who *ought* not to have led the citizens of the *borough* into peril; but all were now *knit* together by this new blessing of peace. They who had *fought* side by side, numerous as *gnats*, collected in *knots*, and talked of the *gherkins* they had *bought* or sold. Gardening *knives*, and sticks with *knobs*, were the only weapons now exhibited. They listened to any suggestions of rebellion with as much dislike as the early Christians felt in listening to the teaching of the *Gnostic* heretics, or a bankrupt when he hears the proposals of his *assignees*. War was a *gnome* which haunted them with terror; and when the *light* of day at length faded, they went *straight* to their cottages, with no *design* except that of sleeping soundly. No fear was there now of being awakened by *neighing* horses, or being *caught* and ordered to case their *thighs* in armor, and then stand on a *height*, as a mark for the enemy, without the

hope of obtaining even a short *furlough*. **The**
knowledge of war had *taught* them all a lesson; and,
as they *knocked* each other on the back with their
knuckles, which some had a *knack* of doing, they
laughed heartily at the recollection of the *danger*
they had escaped.

EXERCISE XVII.

IRREGULAR SOUNDS OF UA, UE, UI.

Laura *Guinness* was born in *Guernsey*. Her
father, who was a stern *pedagogue*, died as he was
haranguing his boys upon the duties of the *deca-
logue*. His widow did not long survive him; and
Laura was then left to the *guardianship* of a man
who was in *league* with a party of *intriguing rogues*
and *demagogues*. Having made himself a *nuisance*
to the Government, he thought it advisable, soon
after Parliament was last *prorogued*, to leave England, and make a *cruise* to *Antigua*, accompanied by
his ward. There they were the *guests* of a noble
general, who was famous in *guerilla* warfare, and
had been a great *conqueror*, and whose property
once belonged to an Indian *Cazique*. Laura's manners were *piquant:* she spoke several *languages*,
and could play a little on the *guitar;* and professed
also to understand the *Eclogues* of Virgil, and had
acquired some knowledge about Mahometan *mosques*.
The General, who, unlike the *roguish guardian*,
was a man without *guile*, and of great *virtue*, though
somewhat *opaque* in intellect, thought she would

prove a *suitable* wife. He gave her *bouquets*, and took her for *picturesque* walks; but his attentions might be termed *oblique* rather than direct, for he did not venture upon any particular *dialogue* until one evening when they met at a *masquerade*, and Laura, after dancing a *quadrille*, and making the *circuit* of the room, was refreshing herself with a *biscuit* and *fruit*. The General then begged her to *guess* his wishes. Laura professed to be under the *guidance* of the *guardian*, and turned the conversation by asking for some lemon *juice* and water. The General, in *pursuance* of his object, *pursued* the guardian, and found him partaking of the plentiful *victuals* provided for the party. He mentioned the amount of *guineas* which he had stored up in *exchequer* bills; produced a *catalogue* of the *antique* jewels and *marquetry* which he had inherited from his father, who belonged to the *guild* of Goldsmiths; and offered to give any *guarantees* that might be *required* for the truth of his statement. In the end, his *suit* was accepted; but Laura, who was as giddy as a *harlequin*, proved herself a sad *coquette*. She *continued* to *coquet* even after her engagement. Her dress was so *grotesque* as to be a subject for constant *critiques*. Her *tongue* was never silent: her manners were *brusque;* and she turned every thing into *burlesque*. Against the General's wishes, she joined in some private theatricals, and, appearing in the *casque* of a warrior, spoke the *prologue* and *epilogue* to the play; and, at length, being urged on by *colleagues* worse than herself, she brought her

self into difficulties from which it was almost impossible to *rescue* her.   The general's heart was
sorely *bruised.*   He gave up all his former *pursuits,*
and devoted himself to Laura, in the hope of *rescu-
ing* her from her foolish companions.   The only
guerdon he asked was, that she should observe the
etiquettes of society.   But all was in vain.   On a
bright morning, Laura was married to a young *re-
cruit ;* and the poor old general, after shedding tears,
plentiful as the streams which *disembogue* themselves
through the *sluices* of a floodgate, or pour through
the hollow cavity of a *conduit,* died of a broken
heart.

EXERCISE XVIII.

H, P, AND W SILENT.

Sarah Groves was the *daughter* of a *sempstress.*
As a child she learnt to *write* a good hand, to read
the *psalter,* to sing *psalms,* and practise *psalmody*
generally.   She could also make *raspberry* vinegar,
according to a *receipt,* and understood the *symptoms*
of illness so as to concoct *ptisans* and *rhubarb* mix-
tures for persons afflicted with *rheums, rheumatism,*
or other maladies.   But her uncle, a rich, *honest*
man, made her his *heiress ;* and then Sarah changed
very much, forgot her care for the *wretched,* and
fancied she was a scholar, and, although as dull as
a *rhinoceros,* imagined it would be more *honorable* to
talk about *rhetoric, rhomboids, rhyme,* and *rhythm,*
than to *wrap* up medicines for the poor.   Yet she
was but a silly, *wriggling* girl, with a *wry* neck and

a *wrinkled* forehead; and she had no more sense than a *ptarmigan*. As in these days there are no *sumptuary* laws, she dressed *sumptuously*, wore *wreathes* in her hair, and spent a fortune in a lotion made of *myrrh;* and, because she had heard of *Psyche*, could spell *psychology* and *rhodedendron*, and knew the names of the *Ptolemies* and the history of the *pseudo*-Smerdis, besides being able to distinguish an *isthmus* from the river *Thames*, she supposed that she knew enough to *answer* all purposes in life. She married a man named *Thomas*, a *writer* in a magazine. He had begun life as a *shepherd*, and afterwards became an *hostler;* but, being clever, he attracted notice by *writing* a poem upon a *wreck*, which, though rather *rhapsodical*, was much admired, and he was admitted as an *honorary* member of a learned society. *Sarah* and her husband went to the *Rhine* for their wedding tour; and, *when* they returned, *Thomas* joined the *Rifle corps*. But his happiness was *wrecked* by his marriage. His wife treated him very *wrongly*, and tried to *wrest* all power from him. In her *illhumor*, she one day called him *sirrah*, and he in return said, *pshaw!* From that hour, they sought to *wreak* vengeance on each other. They *wrangled* continually, and kept up a constant *wrestling* match in words. No one saw the means of *redemption* from such a condition. But one day Sarah was seen at an open window, dressed in *dishabille*, *wringing* her hands, and crying *ah!* loudly. Her husband stood by, holding the scabbard of a *sword*

which he had *wrenched* from her.   No one ever
knew what had happened : but Sarah caught a dan-
gerous *catarrh*, which ended in *asthma ;* and illness
wrought so great a change in her, that she is now
as gentle as a *wren*, and *owns* herself to be, what
she really is, an *empty-headed* simpleton.

EXERCISE XIX.

WH SOUNDED LIKE W AND H.

Young *Whittaker* was playing *whist* last night till
quite late, declaring that he had too much *wit* to
care a *whit what* his aunt, who is a *widow*, would
say : but a boy was set to *watch ;* and, *when* her step
was heard, there was a *whoop*, and the cards *were
whisked* away.   The old lady is certainly full of
whims.   She hates *whistling* and *whispering*, and
cannot bear the *whiff* of a cigar.   She *wastes* her
affections on a *white, whining, wheezing* poodle,
which she has had since it was a mere *whelp*.   Her
diet is *whimsical.*   She likes rye bread better than
wheat, and *will* not drink *wine*, but begins her dinner with a glass of *whey, which* she says is to *whet*
her appetite ; and she is so *wearisome* in her fidgeti-
ness about health, that one day she thought she
should die, because she had a *whitlow* on her finger.
William Whittaker thinks he can *wheedle* her out of
her money ; but he will scarcely succeed.   He is like
a *whirligig ;* when he talks he is always *whittling
wood*, and he will *wear* a *wig*, which *worries* her.
He is a *Whig* in politics, *which* she hates ; and he is

besides very passionate. One day, he gave the *waiter* at the *Wheatsheaf* Hotel, a cut with a *whip*, which made a *wheal* on the man's arm. Then he is so stupid. He has only just left off trundling a *hoop ;* and the *whole* of last *Wednesday*, he was *watching* the *whirling* and *whizzing* of the *wheels* of the steam-engine near the *wharf*, or else floating about in a *wherry*, or digging *holes* in the sand, or trying to make a *whirlpool* by throwing stones into a pond. He scarcely knows a *whiting* from a *whale :* yet he pretends to understand a great deal about the migration of fishes, whence they come, and *whither* they go, and *whether* the *weather* has an effect upon them ; and, in fact, all the *whys* and *wherefores* of their movements. But he is *wholly* a sham, *whom*, I am persuaded, his aunt despises ; and *whose* chance of her property is not *worth* a *whortleberry*.

Exercise XX.

SIMILAR SOUNDS OF CIEN, CION, SIAN, SION, TIAN, AND TION.

A fatal quarrel lately took place between a *Russian* officer and a *Prussian* nobleman. It seems that the former, wishing for some *diversion*, proposed an *excursion*, with the *participation* of several friends. His *proposition* was to take some *provisions*, and a *sufficiency* of wine ; and, on the Monday after *Ascension Day*, to climb a mountain famous for rare *gentians*. Further *suggestions*, and a revision of plans caused an *alteration* in these *intentions ;* and, in the course of *conversation,* the Prussian nobleman fell into a *passion,* and made an *insinuation,* that the *expedition* resembled a barbarian *invasion.* The Russian, in *perturbation,* insisted on the Prussian's *secession* from the *party ;* but, though the latter apologized for his *transgression,* he refused *submission.* *Intercession* failed to produce *reconciliation ;* and as the Russian could not use *coercion,* he had only the *satisfaction* of making a *separation,* and forming a *coalition* against the Prussian. A *portion* of his friends, disliking their *position,* again strove by *persuasion* to effect the *cessation* of the Russian's *indignation.* A *fusion* of the parties would, they said, be more agreeable than a *dispersion* in opposite *directions,* and it was not the conduct of *Christians* to refuse *propitiation ;* besides, the *diminution* of their numbers would be a public *confession* of their want of *discretion.* But the *perversion* of the Russian officer's mind made him persist in the *retention* of his first *decision,* the *retractation* of which would, he asserted, be too great a *condescension,* after such false *asseverations* and *presumption.* *Compassionating* your *impatience,* and to avoid *circumlocution,* I will only add, that the Russian officer gave a *commission* to a friend to carry a challenge to the Prussian nobleman. They met the next morning. The Russian, wearing *Hessian* boots and a *fustian* jacket, arrived first, and took *possession* of the ground. The delay was a trying *probation ;* but the Prussian nobleman soon appeared. After mutual *recrimination*, both were about to fire, when the *reverberation* caused by the accidental *percussion* of one of the pistols, brought to the ground a *missionary* to the *Circassians*, who had a *suspicion* of the affair, though but a slight *comprehension* of the circumstances. His *intervention* had a peaceful *fruition;* but the *tension* of nerves had been too much for the Prussian nobleman. A *suffusion* of blood, followed by *convulsions*, brought him to the verge of death. A *session* of *physicians* was held; and the *incision* of the lancet caused an *effusion*, which for a time relieved him. He was able then to enter into a *discussion* as to the *cession* of his property, and the *succession* of his heir. With careful *prevision*, he made a *provision*, for the *reversion* of his landed estates, and gave *permission* for the *conversion* of his personal property into cash. He also made *mention* of the *remission* of certain debts; so that no *apprehension* might be entertained of any *oppression* from the *discretionary* powers left to his trustees. He spoke of the challenge with much *contrition*, and made loud *lamentations* over the *delusion* which, in accordance with the *conventionalities* of society, had induced him to accept it. He begged that his son might be brought up in *seclusion*, and under careful *tuition;* and added, that he hoped he might thus obtain a *proficiency* in his studies, and, by the *infusion* of good principles, and the *observation* of the *progression* of *civilization*, learn to avoid the *ancient illusion*, which had led mankind to the *deification*

5

of a false honor, although aware of its *insufficiency* as regarded the *preservation* of peace.   These were his last words.   A long *procession* followed him to his grave; and the feeling of anger against the Russian, added to the *inefficiency* of the police, and a *deficiency* in their numbers, nearly produced an *insurrection.*

Exercise XXI.

CI, CY, SI, AND SY SOUNDED ALIKE.

I have been *sitting* with *Sinclair* under the *sycamore* and *cypress* trees, watching the *cygnets* in the pond, and the gardener *syringing* the plants.   Sinclair wished me to praise his cousin *Cyril's* writings; but, though I detest being *cynical,* I cannot be a *sycophant.*   Cyril's *style* is as frothy as *syllabub.* He uses abstruse terms, but they are only connected *syllables;* he does not understand their meaning. He calls a *circle* a *cycle,* talks of reasoning *synthetically,* and argues about *synopsis* and *syllogisms;* but he does not know that the plural of *synthesis* is *syntheses,* and the plural of *synopsis, synopses.*   So again, he thinks he has the learning of a *cyclopædia,* because, instead of employing easy words, he chooses long ones which are, he supposes, *synonymous.*   For instance, he uses *sylvan* for rural, *symphonious* for melodious, *symmetrical* for regular, *synchronism* for a concurrence of events, *syncope* for faintness.   In his book, he talks not of the meaning, but the *significance,* of the *systematic* rules of *syntax;* and inserts *silly* notes on Jewish *syndics* and *syna-*

gogues, and the *cylinders* found in the *Assyrian* ruins. As for *symbolism* and *synods*, about which he talks so absurdly, they are *symptomatic* of the age, and persons who have no *sympathy* with the *system* to which they belong, fancy, nevertheless, that they cannot be *silent* upon them.

Exercise XXII.

PH SOUNDED LIKE F, OR ELSE SILENT.

Mournful were my *feelings* when I drove in my *phaëton* to see the *porphyry cenotaph* of my old friend *Stephen Fowler*, and strove to *decipher* his *flattering epitaph*. The *catastrophe* which occasioned his death was brought *forcibly* before me. I knew that the wisdom of the best *physicians*, the knowledge to be acquired from the *pharmacopœia*, or the *pharmaceutical* experience of the most renowned apothecaries, and the care of men most skilled in *pharmacy*, could not have prolonged his life; for *hydrophobia*, like *phthisis* and the *phthisical* maladies, in which suffering is caused by the accumulation of *phlegm*, is a disease but little understood. But as memory recalled his fine *physiognomy*, his *philanthropic* character, and the *fame* of his *philological* and *philosophical* discoveries, I said to myself, It is no *false phraseology* which thus declares, in *emphatic* though *metaphorical phrases*, that he is a loss to both *hemispheres*. Such a *phœnix*, standing as a *pharos* to enlighten the world, is indeed a *phenomenon*. Gentle as a *nymph*, his words *flowed* with the sweetness of the song of *Philomel*, and the rapidity of the *flight* of a *pheasant*. He might have been deemed *phlegmatic*, but for the *flashing* of his *sapphire* eyes, which kindled as suddenly as *naphtha* or *sulphur*, and shono with the brightness of *phosphorus* whenever he *apostrophized philosophy*. Some, indeed, dared to utter *philippics* against him. A *phalanx* of *flagitious*, *sophistical*, and *pharisaical fools*, *famous* only for *farcical* attempts at *geographical* and *topographical* essays, full of faults in *caligraphy* and *orthography*, to say nothing of errors in *typography*, brought accusations against him, which to repeat would be *blasphemy* against virtue. They termed him a *sophist*, and said he resembled those *amphibious* animals who belong neither to land nor sea. They decried his lectures on *phonics ;* laughed at his hints on *philology*, the origin of *dipthongs*, and the meaning of *periphrasis* and *paraphrase ;* and would not notice his essays on the *phenomena* of *phlogiston*, or his suggestion as to the use of *camphor* in infectious fevers having been known to the later *Pharaohs*. But theirs were the *sophisms ;* his was the *triumph*. He stands as the *hyphen* connecting *physiology* and *metaphysics*. Alas, that there should have been no *philtre* to preserve the life of such a man ; that *phlebotomy* should have failed to save him ; and that nought should now remain of him but the model of his skull, taken by a *phrenologist*, and the *photograph* with his *autograph* beneath, to be seen at the *Photographic* Gallery !

Exercise XXIII.

SC SOUNDED LIKE C, AND S; AND SCH LIKE S AND SH.

You ask me to relate *succinctly* my *reminiscences* of my *predecessor* in office. He was a *civilian*, a *scion* of an ancient family, once the owners of the *Scilly* islands, but whose *descendants* have of late years been *reduced* to merely *decent* poverty. Whilst dining with a barrister on the *circuit*, he died of *ossification* of the heart, or, as some have thought, of an internal *abscess*. I have *ascertained* that his *domicile*, when his talents were first brought into *publicity*, was in a *crescent* in the *vicinity* of *Sion* House, at the *entrance* of the city. It has been *asserted*, that, before the period of *adolescence*, he had *elucidated* the *circle* of the *sciences*, written an essay on the style of art called the *renaissance*, and could discourse upon *indiscerptible* atoms; but this is an *assumption*. Sparks of *transcendent* wit and *similes* worthy of *citation* were indeed often · *elicited* from him; but they were *evanescent scintillations*, the *remembrance* of which was soon *effaced :* and this early *efflorescence* of cleverness, though very *fascinating*, *proceeded principally* from the *effervescence* of youthful *excitement*. His *miscellaneous* information was, however, great; and his *witticisms* were, no doubt, *felicitous* in expression. They cut like *scythes* and *scissors*, and pierced like the pain of *sciatica* or the stroke of a *Damascene scimitar*. The keenness and *delicacy* of his perceptions might have been compared to the *scent* of a hound, or the touch of the elephant's *proboscis:* and, although he was both *susceptible* and *irascible*, and was *conscious* of holding in his hands the *sceptre* of *criticism*, he *exercised* such self-*discipline* that the *oscillations* of his feelings were never *discernible;* for he always remained outwardly in *quiescence*, never moved a *muscle* of his countenance, and rarely committed a *solecism* in *civility.* He was no *ascetic ;* and, as he doomed himself to *celibacy*, he sought the *solace* of *society;* yet there was *certainly* a tinge of *acerbity* in his manner, and his views were *circumscribed*, though he dogmatized as if *omniscience* and *prescience* belonged to him. He seldom *condescended* to *notice* the arguments of his *disciples ;* and I have witnessed many *scenes* in which he behaved no better than a *rhinoceros.* His principles were, upon the whole, *conscientious;* yet his plans, which were merely the immature *excrescences* of his genius, may now be considered not only dead, but in a state of *putrescence.* Even if they were *renascent* for a time, they could never be wholly *resuscitated*, and would soon be *superseded* by others. I cannot, therefore, *rescind* my opinion, or *acquiesce* in your wish that his party and mine should *coalesce.* We have n/w the *ascendency ;* and with such *discordance* between their views and ours, on the subject of the Reform Bill, and particularly the first *schedule*, it is easy to *discern* that the attempt would force us to *descend* from this high position, and would only end in a wider *schism.*

THIRD SERIES.

LETTER I.

FROM A. B. TO C. D.

ASHFORD HALL, February, 1865.

My dear Friend, — I write with an *aching* heart, and make no *apologies* for *abruptness*. The uncle with whom I lived has died of *apoplexy;* and, to *augment* my grief, my *artful* cousin inherits the property, and I am reduced from a state of *affluence* to a small *allowance*. It is an *awful* and *appalling* event. No one was in *attendance* upon my uncle, except his constant *attendant Andrew*. But no *aid* would have *availed*. My uncle was as *abstemious* as an *ancient ascetic* or an *anchorite*. He had once been *athletic*, but latterly he was much *attenuated*. One day, he forgot *abstinence*, and *ate* some *anchovies*, and the doctors *allege* this as the cause of his death. I, however, *attribute* it to the fact, that he had long been *ailing*, and had lately suffered much from *asthma* and an *aguish* fever, and *also* from an *abscess*, the *agony* of which nothing could *allay*. All *anodynes* failed. Taken *all* together, these *ailments* made him *altogether* miserable. He lived, besides, in *apprehension* of *accidents;* but his chief dread was *aneurism* of the heart, of which many of his *ancestors* had died. He was devoted to *arts* and *artists*, espe-

[71]

cially the Royal *Academicians ;* and he had himself great *abilities,* and had won high *academic* honors at Cambridge. I think his death was *accelerated* by the labor of writing a book on the *Accidence* of the English language, particularly the use of the *auxiliary* verbs, and the different modes of *accentuation.* The *accuracy* of this book is remarkable. It has been *abridged,* and I will send you the *abridgment.* I feel deeply *aggrieved,* and cast into an *abyss* of sorrow by this event. I am not *avaricious ;* I have no desire for *aggrandizement,* and no *artificial* wants. I have an *abundance* of *acquaintances,* and many *appointments* are open to my *acceptance.* I should have liked the *artillery* service, but I am too old for it ; and I would rather be an *artisan* than an *attorney :* the law is not in *accordance* with my feelings, and has no *attractions* for me. I must *accommodate* myself to my new life by degrees. Perhaps I may take an *agency :* but at present I feel an *abhorrence* of this place, and long to make myself an *absentee,* or even an *alien ;* yet I am not really *alienated* at heart, and could never give up my *allegiance* to the Queen. If report speaks *aright,* the furniture will be sold by *auction,* and the *auctioneer* has *already* had orders *about* it. I pine for *adventures* and an *adventurous* life, and am *ashamed* to *acknowledge* that the natural *acerbity* of my temper is *aggravated* by the sight of the *ancestral* home, not an *acre* of which will ever be mine. I should like to *achieve* fame by entering the *army ;* but the opportunities of warlike *achievements are* rare ; and to

accoutre myself is impossible, the cost of *accoutre-
ments* being so great.   I detest all *abstruse* studies
except *astronomy*, and have long since *abjured* commerce.   To *ascend* Mont Blanc, or wander *amidst*
the *aborigines* of *America*, will *alone assuage* my
regret.   In fact, I am inclined to *anathematize* certain persons, and feel an *absolute antipathy* to every
one but yourself.   Our tastes have *always assimi-
lated*, and you have often *administered* true consolation in *affliction*.   *Adieu.*   A. B.

I have been *asked* the derivation of *andiron;* can
you give it me?

LETTER II.

FROM C. D. TO A. B.

LONDON, February, 1865.

My dear Friend,—I am *aghast* at your *announce-
ment*, and could not give my *assent* to your departure, even though you were an *adept* in travelling,
and could make the *ascent* of Mount *Ararat* or
Mount *Atlas*.   Are your expectations quite *annihi-
lated?*   Have you not even an *annuity?*   Your
uncle had *amassed* wealth.   I am *amazed* that, with
your *agreeable* and *amiable* disposition, and your
extreme *affability*, which he so greatly *applauded*,
he has left you none.   Some wrong *agency* has been
at work.   Did you ever *affront* him?   Could any
person have been *animated* or *actuated* by feelings
of secret *animosity against* you?   Had you no open
adversary?   I cannot *acquiesce* quietly in the idea,
that nothing of what has so long been your home

now *appertains* to you. The idea is *apparently* an impossibility, *almost* an *absurdity;* for you *always* had your uncle's *approval.* There is some *ambiguity* in your letter. To what do you *allude*, when you speak *angrily* of certain persons? Pray *answer* me. With your *abilities*, is there no *alternative* but that of *absconding*, as it were, *abandoning* your country and going *abroad?* You might find some *advantageous* opening by means of an *advertisement*, or you might make *application* to some *ambassador* or *alderman. Apart* from my wishes, I fear it will not *agree* with you. My *anxiety* will be great during your *absence.* Whether *afloat* or *ashore*, *any* storm will *affright* me for you. You must have some one to *advise* you, and you must take *advice.* Circumstances may seem *adverse* now, but they will *alter.* If I could think of *aught* that would *aid* you, I should rejoice. But you ought not to *absent* yourself I am sure. As soon as the ship had parted from its *anchorage* and weighed *anchor* you would regret it, unless a friend could *accompany* you. If I could go with you myself, I should have *attained* the *acme* of happiness. I have nothing to tell you, except that London swarms like an *ant-hill*, and that my *aunt's* son is now an *accomptant* in Mr. *Alexander's* office. He was ill, but has been cured by *aconite.* If he would only give up *alcohol* he would do well; but this habit produces many *ailments:* he loses his taste for natural *aliments*, his brains become *addled*, he cannot *add* up a sum in *addition*, or tell what are the *aliquot* parts of a

pound. Adieu. Send me your *address* in London.
Yours, *affectionately,*   C. D.

P.S. — Have you seen *Annesley's* book on the
antediluvian history of the earth, and the *anti-Christian* spirit of the *age?* It proves that the *aspersions*
cast upon him are groundless, and I feel sure no
one will *attempt* to *asperse* his character *again,* or
to *assail* with *abuse* a man who is not *assailable.*
Arthur Agar's volume on *annular* eclipses is also
interesting ; and there is a book, I forget by whom,
about *alligators* and *amphibious animals,* and the
animalculæ connected with them, which would be
an *acquisition* to your travelling library. Send me
home an *acanthus* leaf, if you come *across* the plant.
Remember when you write not to use *abbreviations.*
It is an *affectation* which makes me feel *atrabilarious,*
— *alias* cross.

LETTER III.

FROM A. B. TO C. D.

ASHFORD HALL, February, 1865.

My dear Friend, — The *attraction* of the *American* prairies, as well as of the *alluvial* deposits of
Egypt, has been overcome by the *azure* skies of
Italy, and the *antiquities* of Roman *amphitheatres.*
My delight in the *antique,* especially in *architecture,*
and my fondness for *architectural* and *archæological*
studies, *approximate* to a passion. The sight of
the Claudian *aqueduct* will make *amends* for the
anguish I have lately suffered. The *atmosphere* of
Italy, and its *associations,* will soothe me : I look

forward to the country as an *asylum.*   The ambiguity of my last note was *accidental :* I do not
know that any one in particular has been an *acces-
sary* to my disappointment, though several persons
who have at various times behaved *atrociously* and
abominably, and have spoken of me with *acrimony,*
had *access* to my uncle, and were *assiduous* in *amusing* him by *anecdotes,* and I fear took *advantage* of
this free *admittance* to induce him to *alter* his will.
  The *administratrix* of his affairs would naturally
be my aunt, the widow of *Admiral Ainsworth.*
She has lately had an *accession* of fortune, and I do
not think she would have *abased* herself to be the
abettor of any unfair *act.*   She says that my uncle
received *audacious anonymous* letters which *agitated*
and *annoyed* him ; but I cannot *actually ascertain*
the *fact.*   The letters were always left in the *ante-
chamber.*   They *arrived* about 9, A.M., or *ante-meri-
dian.*   One of my uncle's *arrangements* was to keep
an *alphabetical* list of the *addresses* at the end of
an *almanac.*   I, being his *amanuensis,* wished to
have this list made more *accessible,* and I *asked* him
to give it me.   This made him *angry,* and he *ad-
monished* me as if I was still in the *age* of *adolescence,* and I cannot *acquit* him of unkindness *afterwards ;* though, *anterior* to this period, he *abounded*
in *affection* towards me.   I think he must latterly
have had some *aberration* of mind ; for he used to
think that persons were hiding behind the *arras,*
and could see him through an *aperture* in the wall
of the *apartment.*   My aunt *asserts* and *avers* that

she once heard him say to her son *Anthony,* that *ere* he would make me his *heir,* he would leave his fortune to a Mr. *Eyre,* living in *Ayr,* who had ne'er breathed the same *air* with himself, and was seldom, if *e'er,* in his right mind. If my *aunt* was not the *asserter* of this fact, I should not believe it. My uncle has left some money to be given *away* in *alms,* besides a large sum to found an *adult* orphan school, and to *assist* in *apprenticing* six boys. They are to have a small sum for wearing *apparel* until they are *adults.* All the clothes which *appertained* to him he has given to *Augustus,* or Andrew, his *acute, adroit* and *agile* man-servant, whose right *appellation,* and whose true *antecedents,* I never could learn. My uncle's fortune was *accumulated* by the *agglomeration* of small sums. The *aggregate amount* is about forty thousand pounds; but his *annual* income was often increased by *adventitious* circumstances. *Apart* from myself, I cannot help *admiring* and *approving* of the *addition* he has made to the public charities of the county. I have *alternations* of hope and *abject* despair, as, in *anticipation,* I look to the future. I was an *ass* not to have discovered, as I might have done from *appearances* which *adumbrated* the truth, that my uncle had changed his intentions.

I meant to have consulted Mr. *Alison* on that question of the *assessed* taxes, about which you wrote to me; but he is engaged at the *assizes* this week with a case of *assault,* and has business with Mr. *Anstruther's assignees* next week. He will, however, give me his *assistance.* I know no more of the subject than I do of *algebra.* Mr. * * *'s *assets* are, I hear, considerable. He did not make an *assignment* of his goods. I wish you could see the *autumnal* tints, with the rays of the sun touching them *aslant.* The beauty of Nature is enough to convert an *atheist.* Adieu. Yours ever,   A. B.

P.S. — I have put *asterisks* instead of Mr. * * *'s name; but you will understand whom I mean. He is the same man whose head is rather *awry,* and the *axle-tree* of whose carriage broke when we were driving together; and who made the strange confusion between *axis* with the plural *axes,* and *axes* implements. I think also he did not quite understand the distinction between an *autograph* and an *automaton;* and certainly he was much puzzled when we spoke of the dawn as *Aurora.* You will scarcely believe that *Amelia Addison* is *affianced* to him. They met at an *archery* meeting. He is said to be of an old family, and to have a right to *armorial* bearings; but he looks scarcely *admissible* into society.

LETTER IV.

FROM C. D. TO A. B.

London, February, 1865.

My dear Friend, — I *awaited* the *arrival* of your letter with *ardent* impatience, but you must wait *awhile* before I can answer it *aright,* for I have an *array* of books before me, and am on the point of writing two essays, — one upon the *attempt* lately made to *analyze* Butler's *Analogy*, with a review of *Archibald Armitage's Analysis*, and observations upon the value of *Analogical Arguments;* and the other upon the *anachronisms* of historical novels. I fear it will require more literary *acumen* than I possess to bring forward *apposite* and *appropriate* illustrations, and then to *amplify* them. I have been *actively* employed in searching for them; but *activity alone* is not enough. I am going through the *annals* of several periods; but *annalists* are not always to be trusted. Can you tell me if the discovery of *ammunition* and the practice of *alchemy* belong to the same *age?* Also, I wish to know the names of all the kings who have *abdicated* their thrones. I do not myself *approve* of such self-*abnegation*, but neither do I think that any thing can *abrogate* their claims, though misconduct may *abate* them. If you have an *Annual* Register will you lend it me? It may help me to fulfil the task *allotted* me, and to find the dates of some of the *appanages* of the crown, and understand something about bills of *attainder.* The rate at which, in old times, the people were *amerced,* I cannot discover with certainty. I want an *account* of the Spanish *Armada,* of which I know as little as I do of the habits of the *armadillo.* I shall try the effect of these lectures upon a home *auditory* first; but I do not expect an *attentive audience.*

How I wish I could *assuage* your griefs! The *atrocity* of those who, as it were, lay in *ambush* to deceive your uncle can never be *atoned* for. They must be *arrant* knaves. If I were an *aëronaut*, I should myself like travelling. To look down on the world, like an eagle from her *aerie*, and to see the whole *area* of a country from such an *airy* elevation, though it might *affright* some persons, would not *appall* me. *Aërial* voyages would please me more than *aquatic*, and I should *alight* on the earth with regret, after such an *angelical* expedition. The splendid *alabaster altars*, with the long *aisles* of the cathedrals, will suit your *æsthetic* tastes. Perhaps you will see good specimens of *agate* and *amethyst ;* if so, pray purchase them. I trust that *anarchy* and an *anarchical* spirit will soon disappear from the Continent ; and that *anathemas* will no more be hurled at the *aggressors* of Rome. You will not complain of an *arid* country, as if it were to be your *abiding* dwelling-place, and you can *accommodate* yourself to all circumstances ; but there are many *adjuncts* to comfort which you will miss. Bread is not often *adulterated ;* but the wine of the Continent is *acetous*, and I fear its *acidity* may injure you, as you are *accustomed* to drink *ale*. I dislike *acid* wines myself extremely. The smells also are not *aromatic*. Pray take some *alkali* with you, in case any thing should *ail* you, and let me see you *hale* and strong on your return, which I shall *hail* with delight. Shall you be at Rome on the feast of the *Annunciation ?* Pray do not make yourself *amenable* to remark by *avowedly* owning yourself *averse* from foreign laws. I wish you were going under more favorable *auspices*. This season is not *auspicious*. Let me know if you *adhere* to all your plans. If you have a copy of the Papal *allocution*, do let me have it; only take care that it is *authentic*.

A storm of *hail* fell yesterday, and in closing my window I broke it. I know not how to *appease* my *austere* landlady, of whom I stand greatly in *awe*, for her temper is *awful*. She tells me that panes of glass cost a large sum *apiece*. I quote to her wise *axioms, adages, aphorisms,* and *apothegms,* to convince her that money must be spent; and when, in an *amicable* mood, she *apostrophizes* me in return with warnings taken from the *Apocrypha,* which, by the by, she confounds with the *Apocalypse.*

This storm has destroyed a bed of *anemones,* and injured an *alder*-tree, an *acacia,* an *ash,* and an *aspen*-tree in a friend's garden. I hope your *al-mond*-tree planted last *All-Hallows'* Eve is saved.

I am in an *anomalous* position with my landlady, as, some time ago, I paid for her some *arrears* of rent when she was about to be *arrested.* I often say, that I must *arraign* her before a magistrate, or have an *arbitrator* to settle our *arithmetical* disputes; but I doubt whether any *arbitration* or *arbitrement* would satisfy her. She is very *arbitrary* herself. I think most persons who have *aquiline* noses are so. I threaten her, and tell her I would not *abate* my claim even for an *archbishop,* and that my heart. is hard as *adamant ;* but when she turns *ashy* pale, and *artfully* puts her *apron* to her eyes, and in a touching *attitude,* and shaking her *auburn* ringlets,

6

instead of *arguing, appeals* to my *amiability*, I can
no more *argue*, but *amuse* myself by *alarming* her
with an *amount* of hard words.   What do you think
of *annealed, antepenultimate, autonomy, antithesis,
archetype,* and *antitype,* and, as a climax, *anthro-
pophagi?*   I have brought them all in; and she, in
return, talks of my *abjuration*, meaning objurgation,
and says that she has *allies* in the town, who will
ally themselves with her.   I believe there are some
persons living in the *alleys* who would support her.
Yet really she is an *astonishing* as well as an *absurd*
woman.   In *appearance* she is an *Amazon :* she
studies *anatomy* and chemistry, — at least, she asserts that she does; and talks of the properties of
aquafortis, arsenic, asafœtida, ambergris, asphaltum,
and *antimony*, as fluently as she does of *alum*, though
sometimes she confounds them with *ambrosia* and
amber.   But nothing can make her *aspirate* the
letter " h."   Her voice is *audible* at this moment,
and I must say adieu.   Her favorite metal is *alu-
minium*, and her favorite food *aerated* bread.

Pray let me know if you *adjourn* your departure.
I see that the young *adjutant, Arthur Atkins,* who
was tried for *accidentally* but *awkwardly* hurting a
man's *ankle* with an *awl* or *auger*, which nearly
touched an *artery*, and caused the *abscission* of the
leg, has been *acquitted* by the court-martial, and
that no blame *accrues* or is *ascribable* to him.   He
told his tale *artlessly ;* and proved that he is no
assassin, though he does belong to the *asi ine* species, and is easily led *astray*, and *allured* by foolish

antics from which he ought to keep *aloof*. I hope there will be no *appeal*. The *appellant* would certainly lose his case, and there would be severe *animadversions* upon him. What *adds* to my satisfaction is, that the newspapers would call the weapon an *adze* or an *axe*, which it no more resembled than it did an *arquebuse ;* and said that they were *authorized authoritatively* to state, that the *average* number of *acts* of this kind was very large.

Can you tell me where to find an account of the *Abbess* of St. Hilda in particular, of the *abbots* and *abbacies* of England generally, and of the *archiepiscopal* revenues? Also, do not take it *amiss* that I beg you to state to me exactly what an *amice* is, and what is the office of an *acolyte* in the Roman-Catholic Church? Can you tell me *anything* about the practice of *auricular* confession, and what is now the punishment for *apostasy?* I hope you will not think these very *abstruse* questions. I was asked the other day, why an *ace* in cards was so called, and from whence the flower *auricula* derives its name : can you inform me? There are subjects connected with the Church I should like to talk over with you ; one is the sale of *advowsons, another* the reason why Convocation fell into *abeyance.* Tell me if the Castle of St. *Angelo abuts* on the Tiber ; and what is the size of the statue of the *Apostle* in St. Peter's? Does it *approximate* to the gigantic? *Alas !* how many of my pleasures will be at an end when you are gone, and I cannot *adopt* new ones. I am not *adapted* to change. In fact, *adaptation* of any kind is difficult to me, and I shall always *adhere* to old customs. It will be an *age* before we *again amuse* ourselves with *alliteration*, and puzzle ourselves over *anagrams* and compose *allegories*. Those were pleasures without *alloy; albeit* by no means as unfading as *amaranth.* Have you seen an *article* in an *American* paper on the *astonishing arrogance* and false *allegations* of the English *aristocracy?* Is not an *ambulance* quite a modern invention, and is it not derived from *ambulatory ?*

If you do go to Rome, pray see Guido's *archangel*, and make up your mind about the points of history which are doubtful, especially those which concern the Etruscan *augurs* and *auguries.* Adieu. Yours ever,   C. D.

Should "yours" be written with an *apostrophe?*

LETTER V.

FROM A. B. TO C. D.

PARIS, February, 1865.

My dear Friend, — You *bade* me write, saying that letters would be a *balsam* to your spirits during my *banishment.* Indeed I feel that I am *banished, bereaved,* or, as you would say, *bereft,* in this *brilliant Babel* of Paris. I *bewail* my fate; and yet I *breathe* more freely, and there is a certain *buoyancy* in my spirit, which, though it can never *bring back* my past *blithesomeness,* yet makes the *bustle* and *business* of a great city, and the *buzz* of the *busily* engaged people, who seem to *be* as *busy* as *bees, better* for my *blighted* life than the *barrenness* of a house in the country. The visits of the *Baron* and *Baroness* de —— have *been beneficial* to me. The *Baron* wears the *badge* of the Legion of Honor. He is a man of great *beneficence,* and the number of persons *benefited* by his *benefits* is surprising : in fact, he is a general *benefactor ;* and his *benign* words are like *balm* to the sorrowful *bosom,* and must operate *beneficially* on all. Persons reduced to *bankruptcy* and *beggary by* the misfortunes which have *befallen* them, *besiege* his doors, *bemoaning* their fate, and *beseeching* his aid ; and if they are proved to be *blameless* of dishonest *bargains* and of *barefaced* fraud, and have not *been borrowing* upon false pretences, they are sure of *being* assisted. His *biography* would, I am sure, be a *blessing* to the world, for his life is like a sermon on the *Beatitudes. But* I must be *brief,* and turn from the *bountiful* Baron, and only add that his wife is *beauteous* in person, and dresses *beautifully.* She wore the other day a kind of *bombazine,* the color of *beet-root,* with a *brannew bonnet* of the newest fashion. I *believe* my sister will join me here. She has never *beheld* any country but her own ; and *by and by,* when I feel *better,* I shall show her all that this *bewitching* city can offer : but now I must go to *breakfast.*

My *bedroom* looks like a *boudoir,* and opens upon a *balcony,* with a gilded *balustrade,* fronting some handsome *buildings.* I have just been standing there watching a *balloon* go up, which looked no larger than a *bladder.* I always had a *bias* in favor

of the French; you will remember our *boyish bick-
erings* on the subject, and how I found no *blemishes*
in them, whilst, in your deep *bass* voice, you pronounced the whole nation to be *base.* That was
when we lived in a house on the *brow* of the hill,
near the *borough* town of *Bedford,* and made *burlesque ballads* about the old *burghers.* Do you
remember the *burglary* which took place, and the
bootless search after two *brindle* cows which were
stolen when *browsing* in a field? What *banquets*
we had with the officers of the *battalion,* in that
curious *banqueting*-room of theirs in the *barracks!*
and what merry games of *billiards!* Do you recollect how *bashful* you were, and how *boastful* I was?
Some thought our evenings *bacchanalian;* but there
was no *brawling,* though there might have *been*
some *bragging* about *bravery.* Young *Benjamin
Beresford* was the only *braggart* or *braggadocio;*
but he could not *bamboozle* me : I always hated his
basilisk look. I heard the other day, that he *behaved
brutally* when *besieging* a town in India. *Bombshells*
were cast into it, which *burst,* and killed many in
the *beleagured* town ; and a *battery* of guns was
turned against it, which soon made a *breach.* It
was *bloody* work ; and, though it is scarcely *believa-
ble,* Benjamin would not give the inhabitants time
to *bury* their dead. He is, in fact, only a *bully* and
a *buffoon,* and has shown by his *brutal behavior*
that he is not worthy of the name of *Briton,* but is
more like a *brute beast;* and Great *Britain* may
well be ashamed of his *barbarity* and *brutality.* He

is, I hear, quite *bloated, bulky,* and *blear-eyed,* and his face is *blurred* with *blotches.* I should like to give him the *bastinado.*

But all this is mere *bagatelle.* I must turn to *business.* I wrote to you the other day about the *bureau* you are to keep, and I hope you will obey my *behest.* My grandfather *bequeathed* it to me. It was his only *bequest.* He left it me just *before* he *breathed* his last *breath,* giving me also his *benison* in words, the *brevity* of which did not surprise me, as he was suffering from *bronchitis,* and the *bronchial* tube was much diseased. In this bureau, you will find the *balance* of my last year's allowance, with a specimen of gold *bullion,* also two *brooches,* a *buckle* of *burnished* gold, a Latin *breviary,* a *botanical book* called " Lectures on *Botany,*" a view of the *Baptistery* of Pisa, some *bills,* and a *board bored* with holes for a new kind of game, which I was tempted to *buy,* but which, *by the by,* I never learnt to play; also a *backgammon* board, and a *bronze bell,* given me by Miss *Belinda Barrington,* the *belle* of the *ball* at *Bridport.* Ah! what a happy evening that was, and how we sat under the *boughs* of the *beech* trees the next day, and admired the *boll* of the great *birch,* and sauntered along the *beach!* I, who was then buoyed up with hope, have now no one to *befriend* me.

That word *boll* reminds me of the story told by the *Bishop* of *Beverley* to one of his Episcopal *brethren,* of his first visit to France. He asked for *beef* tea: they brought him a *brimming bowl* of *bluish* liquid, which they called *bouillon,* and which he found to be *barley* water. Things are better now. If I could get good *Bohea* tea, *bacon, biscuits, batter* pudding, and *Bannock* cakes, I should do well. The *butter* is good, but the water is *brackish.* I fear I shall *become bilious,* unless I can drink *bitter* ale. I try to think, that, with regard to *bodily* comforts, I am not worse off than if I were *bivouacking ;* and I hope I am *beginning* to be more contented with my present *berth.* But I still sigh for the land of my *birth.* I had a *bullet* given me yesterday, which was picked up at one of the *barricades* during the last Revolution. I have been reading a novel which is half *blasphemous,* half *bigoted.* Of course, you will know it does not suit me. I am no *bigot,* indeed I detest *bigotry.* This weather makes me think of *batting* and *bowling,* and the delight of a *bath* afterwards. They say it is as hot here as on the coast of *Barbary,* and dogs are going mad. A man was *bitten* yesterday, and has since died of the *bite.*

I did not *broach* a word of my probable long absence to my aunt when I said good-*by,* but made her believe that I was *bent* on returning. She was preparing for my cousin *Beatrice's bridal.* Beatrice herself *beckoned* me to her, *bridled* and *blushed,* twisted the *bobbin* which fastened her *boddice,* made me a kind of *bobbing* curtsey, *begged* me to look well after my *baggage,* gave me some *briony* which she held in her hand, and then bade me farewell, little thinking how long it would be *before* we could live again *beneath* the same roof. How pretty she looked

with her *braided* hair! though I used to call her
nose a *beak*, and say it would serve for a *beacon*.
We had been together since we were *babies*, and we
cried at the sight of a *beetle*. Hers has always *been*
a most *blameless* life. I wish any one could speak
as *blamelessly* of mine. She had a fancy to have
her *banns* published, and so it was done. Her
prospects are *blissful*. Her intended husband is
a *brave* soldier, but very *bald*, and with the mark
of a *bruise* on his cheek from a wound given him
by a *bandit*, who had a large troop of *banditti* following him. He is so deaf that the service must,
I am sure, be *bawled* in his ears to make him hear
it. The *bridesmaids* are to wear *buff*-colored
dresses. I gave Beatrice a *beautiful* pearl pin, with
the pearls clustered together like *blackberries*. But
I must have *bored* you with all this nonsense. I
believe I was *born* to *bore* people; and I fear I shall
do so till I am *borne* on my *bier* to my grave, having
reached the *bourne* from whence no traveller re-
turns. Do not make a *butt* of me, but *bear* with
me; for I am *bare* of comfort and solitary as a *bit-
tern*, and at times I feel as fierce as a *bear* or a wild
boar. If I had been *bred* up as a *boor*, I should
have been used to earn my *bread*, but this reverse
of fortune *breaks* my heart, and my *breast* is heavy
with care. I talk of going to *Brest;* but I care not
whether I visit the *Bay* of Naples, or the *Bight* of
Benin, or pay a visit to the *Bey* of Tunis.

If I could but mount my *bay* horse, and ride
through the *bushy brakes* of *brier* to the *boundary*

of my uncle's estate, how *blest* should I be! The life of a *borderer* always charmed me, but I have been *balked* of all such joys. You used to *badger* me, and say my character wanted *ballast*, and needed *bracing*, and that I was a mere *babbler;* and, like a boy, *buoyed* myself with hopes founded on false reports, or, as you called them, *bruits.* It was all true. In those days, I was led away by any *bait* which offered itself: opposition excited my *bile;* and I would no more *bate* one jot of my pretensions, than my Paris landlord would one item of his bill. I feel as if a *baleful* and *baneful* influence must have been excited against me, though my efforts to discover the *betrayer* of my hopes have been *baffled.* If you hear of me as a *boatswain* on *board* a ship, do not be surprised. I think to see a ship *bristling* with cannon, and to hear the *booming* of guns, and the whizzing of *bullets* over the *bulwarks*, would alone rouse me.

My sister has *bought* for the youngest boy of Mr. *Bracebridge*, — the *brewer* who *brews* the *bad beer*, a *barrel* of which I once returned, — a hat trimmed with *bows* of *blue* ribbon : it will make the child quite a little *beau.* I would much rather have given him a *ball*; for he is a *bouncing bold* little fellow, though at times he *bellows* and *blusters* till he makes the house like *Bedlam.* I fancy I see him now, *begrimed* with dirt, clinging to the *balusters*, whilst his nurse stood by, her face *blanched* with fear.

The weather is *bleak:* the wind *blew* hard this

morning, and a donkey *brayed* in the court-yard; both which signs, together with the fall of the *barometer, betoken* a change.

I miss the *bellman* much; and I fear I shall be *behindhand*, and shall find no one to be the *bearer* of my letters to the post. It is too *bad* of the waiter not to come, when I *bade* him be careful to remember.

This is as lengthy as a *barrister's brief.* Tell me what is done to the *beadle* who was accused of that *barefaced* robbery of *bales* of *baize* from the *booth* in the fair. Is he allowed to offer *bail?* I should fear his offence is not *bailable.* This *bachelor's* life is not *beatific:* I feel as weak as a *bulrush*, and eat nothing. A *bit* of *brown bread*, were it the color of *bistre*, would be better for me than the *buttered* rolls which they give me; especially if I could have some of the *barberry* jam with it, which I used to enjoy when I was with you at *Bicester.* You may recollect I am as fond of the latter as a South American is of *bananas.* Did you not, when a boy, always confuse bananas with a *banyan* -tree? Tell me whether you were a *better* at the last Epsom races? Also, what is said in England about the foreign *belligerent* Powers and the American *blockade*, and what are the prospects of vote by *ballot?* Farewell. Yours, A. B.

I hear that a *barrow* on one of the Wiltshire hills has been opened, and that *bushels* of *bones* have been found in it. Is that true? Those are the highest hills you have seen; but, if you were *bolder*, you would come with me, and together we would view the *boulders* of the Alps.

LETTER VI.

FROM C. D. TO A. B.

LONDON, March, 1865.

My dear Friend, — To see you *cheerful* under your *checkered circumstances* would *cheer* me *considerably*; but whether you *circumnavigate* the globe, or *continue* within the *circumscribed circle* of your own *country*, I am *convinced* you will never *conquer* your *constitutional* tendency to despondency. What others *consider* a *competency* would not *content* you; for your tastes are not *compatible* with economy. I do not *condemn*, far less do I *contemn* you : I only *commiserate* your *condition*. You *complain*, because you are always *comparing* your *case* with that of others ; and *comparisons* are always *conducive* to discontent. You would be *comparatively* rich, if your desires were *commensurate* with your means. Forgive these *comments*. I would not thus *commence* our *correspondence*, but I *cannot conceal* from myself, that you are full of *chimerical* projects ; whereas, if you would *concentrate* your views on *commerce* and *commercial* employments, you would soon find *cause* for thankfulness. I shall be glad when you have the *companionship* of your sister : such *company* would form the *complement* of my felicity ; but I fear it will not *complete* yours. Pray give her my *compliments*, and *congratulate* her on the *chance* she now has of- seeing foreign *cathedrals* and the *ceremonies* of Roman *Catholicism.* Ask her to find out exactly at what hour *compline* is usually said. It is a *curious coincidence*, that her friends, Miss *Catherine* and Miss *Caroline Cross-thwaite*, are going abroad at the same time. I *confess* I envy you all. I am just *come* back myself from a *committee* of the society for investigating the *corruptions* of *charitable corporations.* I had a *colloquy* with *Charles Cholmondely*, who is as full of *conceit* as ever : I can *conceive* nothing less likely to *conciliate*, than his way of *criticising* other persons' *concerns.* His *criticisms* are *captious* and *concise :* he will *concede* none of his opinions, and his self-*complacency* as to the plan he has himself *concocted* is really *comical.* He told me, that a *Charity Commission* will soon be formed by Government, and that he is to be one of the *commissioners.* He said also, that he had *committed* a mistake in not standing for the *county*, that he should have had no *competitor* for popularity ; for that every one knew it was impossible for any *commoner* to *compete* with him, and therefore *competition* was out of the question. Such self-*consciousness* as his I never saw, and yet at times he is almost *clownish* in manner. He is *certainly* a man of *considerable capacity ;* and, if he spoke with less *circumlocution*, he might be eloquent. *Collegiate* bodies are his aversion, though he was educated at *Caius College, Cambridge.* He began life as *Comptroller* of the *Customs* in Scotland, but lost his situation because he could not *control* his temper.   He then had something to do with the *commutation* of tithes.   My *cousin* was his *coadjutor.*   In some way, which I never could *comprehend,* he was shamefully *cozened ;* and, besides, he *commanded* and *coerced* every one beneath him, as if he had been the *commandant* of a garrison, and made *compulsatory,* and *coercive* regulations with so little *compunction,* that it is to me *incomprehensible* how he ever met with any one sufficiently *complaisant* to bear with him.   Yet he thinks he has a tender *conscience ;* for he cannot bear the *commination* service, and dislikes the *commemoration* of saints, and has *compiled* a new Prayer Book, and edited *Cruden's Concordance :* in fact, I know no one so strange or so *clever* in the whole *circle* and *compass* of my acquaintance.   One thing more I must tell you.   He believes that *comets* are made of *combustible* materials, and, after making the *circuit* of the *concave circumambient* heavens, explode. This is a *closely* written, badly *concocted* letter, but I trust to your *clemency* to pardon it.   Adieu.

Have you heard that we are to have a *coalition* ministry, and that men of the most *discordant* opinions are about to *coalesce ?*   Adieu.   C. D.

LETTER VII.

FROM A. B. TO C. D.

Paris, March, 1865.

My dear Friend, — After a *close confabulation* and *conference* with my sister, I have decided on the *course* to adopt. My sister has been ill, but is now *convalescent ;* and, in order to secure this *convalescence,* she like most other *convalescents,* thinks *change* necessary, therefore we go to Rome for *Christmas.* It will require the *closest* economy, but I have no *choice.* My sister *chose* to go at once, and I could not but *choose* the same. We have had an alarm of *cholera* in this hotel. A very *choleric* old gentleman, who yesterday *committed* an excess in drinking *cider* and eating *citron* pudding flavored with *cinnamon* is a *corpse* to-day. He was united by the *closest* ties of *confidence,* though not of *consanguinity,* to an Indian *civilian,* whose dressing-*closet* opened out of his bed-*chamber,* and who had a knowledge of *chemistry,* and who was famous for *chemical* skill. Through the *chilliness* of night, and the *chillness* of the dawn, and though subject to severe fits of *coughing,* this civilian *conjured* to be allowed to watch by the *cold corse* lying in the *coffin.* He appears to be a *conscientious* man, and the *circumspection* and *civility* of his *conduct* are remarkable. Yet if he were a *conjuror,* trying to *conceal* the arts by which he is able to *conjure,* his *conduct* could not have *caused* more *conjecture, cogitations* and *curiosity.* I have myself *condoled* with him on the loss of his friend, and he has received my *condolences civilly* and *courteously ;* but he will talk to no one but a *clerical* friend, a Mr. *Clarke, curate* of *Cirencester,* who is staying here.

But I must *condense* what I have to say, and *cease* to tire you with a *conglomeration* of news. I wish

I could *confer* with you as to my plans; such a discussion would be the greatest *comfort* to me : you would have *conferred* on me a real benefit by *crossing* the *Channel,* and *coming* to me.   I am reading old *chronicles* and studying *chronology,* and learning the dates of the French kings in the *chronological* order.   My sister says she is leading the life of a *chrysalis* now, but that she shall have a new existence under the *clear circumference* of the Italian skies.   In the meantime she is buying new *clothes* and ornaments ; amongst others a *charming cloak,* and a brooch somewhat in the form of a *chrysanthemum,* made of a *chrysolite, chrysoprasus,* a *carbuncle,* and a *cornelian.*   I have only bought a *chronometer.*

Paris is certainly a most *civilized city.*   The *cleanliness* of the *causeways* is much greater than it used to be, and the *cleanness* of the hotels is charming.   I have never tasted *coffee, chocolate,* or *cocoa,* as good as we have here.   Am I not *correct* in thinking that chocolate is made from the *cacao*-tree ?   In a *chit-chat conversation* I had yesterday with a French friend, the fact was *controverted.* My friend is fond of *controversy,* and is *conspicuous* for the *contradictory conclusions* at which he arrives. In fact, his *chief characteristic* is his *contempt* for the rules of logic !   The *contrariteies* of *character* which are met with in this *cosmopolite* and *corrupt* town are strange.   I hope my principles are not *corruptible ;* but evil is *contagious,* and I might be *contaminated* if I did not feel, that it is nobler *courageously* to bear *contumely* than to allow one's self to be *cheated* by *contemptible counterfeits.* Do not *criticise* the in*coherency* of my language, but lay aside your *customary critical currishness,* and *continue* to think of me as your affectionate friend.

A. B.

LETTER VIII.

FROM C. D. TO A. B.

LONDON, March, 1865.

My dear Friend, — I hoped to receive some *circumstantial* details of your proceedings, but you give me scarcely a *clew* to them ; and, knowing your *changeableness,* I cannot *calculate* upon what you will do. Still you write *cheerily,* though you are *chary* of news. My own mind is just now in a *chaos,* for I have *casually* heard of a *calamity* which adds to the *catalogue* of railway *catastrophes* and *casualties.* A *captain* in a *cavalry* regiment of *cuirassiers* — a man of great *capacity,* and *celebrated* alike for the *circumspection,* the *caution,* and the *celerity* of his movements, which stopped the *carnage* of the *Crimean campaign* — was sitting in the *central compartment* of the *carriage* (he ought properly to have been in the *coupé*), when a *collision* between two trains took place, and a *chaotic* scene of *confusion* ensued. The captain's foot was *caught* in the *circling* wheels, and, as he tried to *cast* himself from the carriage, he was killed. What I think *chiefly characterizes* such accidents is the *consummate carelessness* of the persons concerned. There

7

must be some *check* put upon it.   The poor captain
had a *capital career* open before him : he had a
charming wife and *cherub children,* who were await-
ing him in his home.

A *check* for 500*l.* was in his *coat-pocket,* and, in
consequence of a *Chancery* suit, this is all which his
family have at present, except a few pounds in
the Queen's *current coin.*   His wife suffers from
catarrh ; indeed, all his children are subject to
catarrhal affections.   I hope that, from his *celebrity,*
the *calamitous* affair will be taken up by Government.   The *Chancellor* of the Exchequer has sent
messages of condolence, so I hear from the old *char-
woman* who *cleans* my *chambers,* and who gains her
news from the *chambermaid* of the hotel *close* by.
I am told that the captain might have made a *colossal*
fortune by *chicanery ;* but he would not consent to
do so.   One of his sons has a *salary* in a public
office.   I dined with him last year at a *cheap café*
in Paris, where we drank *champagne,* and ate *chops,
chicken, celery,* and *currant* tart.   Alas for the
chances of life !   How the *current* of the stream
changes !   But to turn to another subject.   I am
collecting particulars about the *cere-cloth* or *cerement*
used by the Egyptians, and also their funereal *ceremonies.*   I mean *cursorily* to describe the *ceremonial*
in an essay, and if you can *contribute* any information you will be doing a *charitable* act.   I hope soon
to be a *contributor* to "The *Cornhill* Magazine,"
but I should much prefer being a "Times" *correspondent.*

A *conventicle* has been opened just opposite to my rooms ; there are *constant* services, and the *customary* singing, which renders its *contiguity* disturbing ; but it is a *consolatory* thought that the *congregation* are satisfied.

I saw *Constance Carey* yesterday, but did not find her *conversible*, though she burst into an *uncontrollable* fit of laughter when I told her that I had mistaken her for *Charlotte Carter*, the *cheesemonger's* daughter. Constance is devoted to *croquet*, and I am *convinced* that, in a quiet way, she would be a *coquette ;* but it is no use to *coquet* with me, for I am devoted to *celibacy*, and *coquetry* has no effect upon me. It may not *criminal*, but it makes me *cynical* and *cantankerous*, and increases my inclination to *cavil* and behave like a *captious curmudgeon.*

Having no *certitude* as to your *contemplated* movements, I shall *commit* this letter to the *care* of your landlord. I used to admire your *caligraphy*, but it has fallen off *considerably ;* no two *consecutive* words are alike. I should like to *consign* you to an instructor, who would inflict on you *condign* punishment for *clipping* your letters so as to make *casuistical* look like *cannibal*, and *canker* like *cancer.* I must *censure* you for this. A *cipher* would even be better ; for, although there might be only a *circuitous* mode of interpreting it, it would in the end be more *certain*, and there would not be the same risk of *confounding* the *censer* used in offering incense with *Cato* the *censor*, or the *census* of a population.

I was present yesterday at the *christening* of the

child of *Christopher Cornwallis.*   Christopher afterwards *catechised* the school-children, who understood their *catechism* well.   This system of *catechetical* instruction is valuable when the *catechist* is *clever.* I suppose it was used with the *catechumens* of the primitive *Church.*   Under any *circumstances,* it is good to teach children to give a *categorical* answer. Christopher wore a *cassock,* and had a *cicatrice* across his *cheek,* which made him look strange.   I hear he has lately given a *chalice* to the church; but I think he is more fit for *classical* studies than for *clerical* duties.   His sermon was on *Christian* baptism, which he *compared* with the rite of *circumcision.*   He spoke also of the use of *chrism* in the Roman - *Catholic* service.   He has the *canticles chanted.*   I heard it said that he was to be the new *canon* of *Canterbury.*   One of my little nephews asked me if that meant he would have any thing to do with *cannons* or great guns, and the other inquired if he would be *canonized,* and I was obliged to explain to him the wide difference between a *canonry,* and *canonization.*   That reminds me of the title of *canoness* in France.   Can you tell me what it means?   Now, farewell.   I wish I could *convey* to you a more *convincing* proof of my affection, or give you wise *counsel;* but every one thinks himself his best *counsellor,* and I am sure that if I could be advanced to the dignity of *councillor,* by being a member of the Privy *Council,* you still would prefer your own opinion.   Adieu.   Yours,   C. D.

LETTER IX.

FROM A. B. TO C. D.

PARIS, March, 1865.

My dear Friend, — You think me *crazy* because I cannot be *contented* like yourself to *creep* and *crawl* like a *caterpillar*, but *choose* to be *capricious* in my movements. You do not mean to be a *calumniator*, but you mistake me. *Certainty* is in my *case* impossible. A *chain* of *circumstances* connects me with other persons, and it is they who are *changeful*. I hoped this very day, that, with the *crowing* of *chanticleer*, I should have left Paris, and have set forth towards the *countries* where I hope to see the *cowls* of *Capuchin* monks, the *cutlasses* of Swiss *carabineers*, the *crowds* who worship in St. Peter's, and the *cardinals* who form the *conclave* and the *consistory* of the Vatican. But unforeseen *contingencies* have delayed me. The *courier* I had engaged has acted *contumaciously;* and, though his *contumacy* did not last long, he expressed so little *contrition* for having neglected to observe an important *clause* in the *covenant* made with me, that I *cordially* disliked him. His character and mine were not *consonant;* and *consonance* is essential in such cases. I have therefore *chosen* another. This man has fingers like birds' *claws*, and a *croaky* voice; he wears *creaking* boots, and *chuckles* to himself when he hears a *capital* joke: but there is nothing really *censurable* about him. I do not doubt

that he will *convoy* us safely to the *Capitol.*   He is
a *Colossus* in stature, and has legs as tall as those of
a *camelopard*, and the *color* of his hair is very nearly
crimson.   I believe he has been in our *colonies;* by
which, however, I do not mean that he is a *convict.*
He went out, I believe, as *cockswain* on board a
French vessel.   He promises to *cater* for us well.
The other man was really a *charlatan:* he pretended
to be a *connoisseur* in art, but he knew nothing.

Your description of Christopher *convulsed* me
with laughter; I should as soon have thought of
seeing him in a *cuirass* or armed *cap-à-pie*, and with
a *casque* on his head like the *commander* of a Roman
cohort, as wearing a cassock.   Pray, where is his
curacy?   Is it not in the *collieries?*   As a boy, I
remember he was *candid* and *contemplative*, and had
a particular fancy for *candied* orange peel and *cura-
çoa.*   He was my *contemporary* at college; his first
year was *contemporaneous* with mine.   In those
days, instead of being tall as a *column*, he was *cir-
cular* as a *cask.*   I remember he told me that his
uncle, who was either a *currier*, a *cordwainer*, or a
cashier in a bank, I forgot which, was subject to
wonderful fits of *coma*, which somewhat resembled
catalepsy, and that for months afterwards he could
not tell the difference between a *comma* and a *colon*,
or a vowel and a *consonant.*   As I speak, it seems
centuries ago.   Can you not remember how we wandered in the *cloisters*, or sat on the old walls gathering the *centaury* which grew on it, and discussing
whether the name was derived from *Centaur;* also,

how we argued about the time of the Roman *calends*, and the meaning of *Candlemas*; and laughed at the man who mistook *calendar*, an almanac, for the art of smoothing linen, which washerwomen call, to *calender*; and how we wandered off then to the bridge of *Callandar*? Christopher's *cachinnation* in those days was like the *cackle* of a duck; and what a *contrast* it was to the *cadence* of the *chimes*! Yet he was learned about the *centrifugal* and *centripetal* forces, and *capillary* attraction, and was besides a *collector* of *curiosities*. He had a piece of *cellular* tissue, which, seen through a microscope, looked like *canvas*. He had also a specimen of *chalcedony*, and a *cork*-model. His words fell like a *cascade* then, and he was always *challenging* his friends to argue with him; but he was as *changeable* as the *chameleon*. When he left college his *chattels* were sold. They *consisted* chiefly of *chairs*, *candlesticks*, and *charts*. But there were also some *candelabra* which were given to the *chapel*, and placed in the *chancel*; one *candelabrum* standing on each side. The *chasteness* of the *carving* was charming. I believe there was a *citation* afterwards from some *court* on account of them; but the *collegiate* authorities *curtly* declined to attend to it. Christopher has been very *contented*, I believe, in his *conjugal* condition. His wife was a *co-heiress*: she was thought to be *consumptive*, and was much *coddled* by her family in *consequence*. I have heard she is very *charitable*: they say, in fact, that her *charities* are enormous. She gives away *counterpanes*, *coverlids*, *clothes, chaldrons* of *coals*, and *caldrons* of *cabbage*-soup.   In fact, her home is quite like a *caravansary.* The whole *carcass* of an ox is said to have been *cut* up and distributed at Christmas.   Her name is always *coupled* with *charity* and *chastity ;* but though she is thus *conspicuous* for virtue, there are those who *construe* her *consistency* into *conceit*, and say that she uses *cosmetics*, and that her rather *ceremonious curtsies* are not *courtesies*, but the *symbols* of a selfish nature.   But I know she regards these reports no more than the tinkling of a *cymbal.*   You will hear what I have said *corroborated* by all who know her.   The *contour* of her face is *captivating ;* and she would be the *cynosure* of admiring eyes, but that her *complexion* is rather *chalky*, and her hair inclining to *carrot*, which prevents her *comeliness* from being *complete.*   She looks best when mounted on a horse, *caracoling* down *Cadogan* Place.   With her husband's *concurrence*, she sold the other day a diamond, weighing I forget how many *carats*, and gave the money to the *Charing-Cross* Hospital.   It is *cruel* to place an action like this under the *category* of pride ; but I believe that there has been a *complete cabal* and *conspiracy* against her amongst her relations, and many persons have been *cajoled* into joining it.   But you will *care* little for all this : my thoughts are turning to the *chamois* of Switzerland, and the *catacombs* of Rome.   When I have seen the *craggy* Alps, the *cupola* of St. Peter's and the *cartoons* of Raphael, I shall be satisfied.   Farewell.   Yours,   A. B.

LETTER X.

FROM A. B. TO C. D.

PARIS, March, 1865.

My dear Friend, — I can get no one to *co-operate* with me in my plans, and I have *cancelled* those which I had made. My sister's *caresses*, — and you know how *caressing* she can be, — have been a *counterpoise* to my own wishes. I do not like to act *contrarily* or *crossly*, and it is decided that we go by the Mediterranean. I have very *crude* notions about this sea, but I doubt much whether it is ever *cerulean ;* and I should like to take *chloroform*, and be under its influence during the voyage. Some say that *camphorated* spirits would be an assistance ; but I should have as much faith in *camomile* tea. I regret losing Switzerland, and especially I wished to see the *confluence* of the Rhone and the Aar. I think of many of my former *companions* in England, who are employed in *collating* manuscripts, *chopping* logic, or even *conjugating* verbs, with envy. I try to *cloak* my real feelings ; but some *chance* word often strikes a *chord* in my heart which awakens almost *convulsive* sorrow. The other day, whilst standing at the entrance of the *choir*, in the Church of St. *Clotilde*, and looking at a *crucifix*, a *chorus* of the *choiristers'* voices burst forth which carried me back to our *choral* meeting. The *cords* of affection which bind me to my country seemed dearer than ever. I thought I should like to be

a *corporal* in an infantry *corps,* or the driver of a
stage-*coach,* or a *clerk* in a *counting*-house ; any
thing so that I might be in England.   My sister
does not participate in these feelings ; she buys *col-
lars* and *cuffs,* and *combs* and *cream* for the hair ;
studies the fashion of every new *coif ;* admires the
costly crockery which she calls *china,* but which is
no more like *Chinese* porcelain than a *cockatrice* is
like a *Charmontelle* pear ; and, in fact, has *carved* out
for herself a *comfortable* life.   The *comfits* which
sicken me, she likes.   Meat burnt to a *cinder,* or as
one may say *calcined,* which *chokes* me, she enjoys.
She does not mind being *curtailed* of *comforts,* and
rejoices in un-*carpeted* floors, and the absence of
cushions.   I think her *cuticle* must be thicker than
mine.   I suppose, however, the real difference is
the *corrosive* sense of disappointment, which *cor-
rodes* every pleasure.   I cannot become *callous,* and
nothing can *countervail* the objection I have to exile.
This *climate* does not suit me : I *cower* over the
fire, and fancy I have *chilblains.*   Remember I am
a perfect *cormorant* for letters.   You will feel for
me, when I tell you that the washerwoman will
crease my *cravats.*   I wish I was less a slave to
corporeal needs ; but really the *crinkles* make me
inclined to *curse* the day when cravats were in-
vented.

   After travelling so much, I think of setting up as
a *cosmopolitan,* and writing an essay on the *cos-
mogony* of the world.   Such *coruscations* of genius
there will be in it !   I shall survey the *cycles* of

ages, and decide upon the age of *coral* reefs and *coralline* formations. I have also some theories as to the *crystalline* humor of the eye, and the *crystallization* of *crystals*, the working of *copper* mines, and the use to be made of *copperas* ; and if I can write *cleverly* of abstract and *concrete*, introduce a few hard words, such as *corpuscles*, *correlative* propositions, *corollaries*, *curvilinear* lines, *contravallations*, *cubical* and *cylindrical* forms, the *cartilages* of the body, and *cutaneous* disorders, I shall be fit to be the editor of a *Cyclopedia*. Alas! the *cypress* will be planted on my grave long before I can return to *carry* out such projects ; but whether I die in *Corinth* or *Cyprus*, or am buried in a *crypt*, or sleep beneath a *carved canopy*, the sounds of my *childhood*, the *curfew*, and the *cuckoo*, will to the last moment of existence be dear to me.

The *cupboard* in my nursery in *Clarendon Crescent*, the little *cubicle* in which I slept, and the *cornice* which ornamented the *ceiling*, are to me more precious than the splendor of the *courts* of the *Czar* and *Czarina*. Do not write me a *critique* upon this effusion. Many forget their *childhood :* it is *contrariwise* with me. I must pass the period of my grand *climacteric*, before I can *cease* to look back to it. I remember how I used to play with the *cows* and *calves*, and to watch the *churning* of butter in the dairy, and the *cartwright* and *carpenter* *cleaving* and *clipping* wood in their yards. I can recall going to the Navy-yard, and seeing the men stopping *chinks*, *caulking* and *careening* the vessels, and making *cables*. I should have thought it no loss of *caste* to have *cast* in my lot with them.   I recollect one day watching two boys amongst them, who were *combatants*, and who struck me as quite *chivalrous* in their *conduct*.   The elder had taken from the younger a *cygnet* which he had *captured*. The *cheeks* of the younger were the *color* of *carmine* or *cochineal*.   But he appealed to the *clemency* of the *conqueror*, and in an instant the *captor* restored his prey.   I was so pleased that I gave the young fellow a little *signet*-ring which I wore.   In those days my chief ambition was to be warden of the *Cinque* Ports, and to head a *confederacy* against tyrants.   When at school, we held formal *sessions* by the light of tallow *candles*, in which subjects like the *cession* of Savoy were discussed.   I am afraid we were rather a *controversial crew*.   How pleasant it was to roam in the *copse*, or, as it was then *called*, the *coppice ;* or even to throw a *crooked* stick into the *creek*, and watch it float !   But all is *changed*.   My *constitutional* sadness is, however, only augmented by writing, so I think I will say adieu.   Yours,

A. B.

Pray send me *Colonel Carter's* book on Roman *Conduits*.   I made a Frenchman spell *colonel* the other day, and of *course* he thought it was *kernel*. Have you lately observed how very clear the *constellation* of *Cassiopeia's Chair* is ?

LETTER XI.

FROM A. B. TO C. D.

PARIS, March, 1865.

My *dear* Friend, —— I am your *debtor* for a *delightful* letter, *doubly* welcome in the *dearth* of *details* from my own *domicile,* and the *dilatoriness* of our *doughty* but far from *docile* courier, who has *detained* us in *duresse* and *dudgeon during* the last week. *Desuetude* makes it *difficult* for me to *do* my *devoir,* and *daunt* him with *denunciations;* and the *douceurs,* of which I am the *donor,* and which he *does* not *disdain* to accept, do not *diminish* his *desultory doings.* Yet, as he is *decorous, disciplined,* and *discreet,* and I *discover* no *defalcations* in money, we do not *decidedly disagree.*

Our *definite determination* now is to *depart* tomorrow. We are to make a *détour* by the *delightful demesne,* or, as we usually write it, the *domain* of Fontainebleau, which *doubtless* will be *delicious during* these *dry days.* My sister needs a *duenna* for the sake of *decorum,* and as she has not one, I am *doomed* to *devote* myself to *dissipation.*

The Parisian *drama* has, I find, *degenerated* and *deteriorated.* There are *dissensions* amongst the *dramatis personæ* of the theatre. They are *dissatisfied* with the *director* of the orchestra, who, being *deaf* and *dyspeptic,* has caused some *dire disappointment* and *disaster.* His *disobligingness, disingenuousness,* and *duplicity,* it is said, must end in *dismissal;* but such *discordancy, diversity, discrepancy,* and *divarication* are found in the *disclosures* of the *despicable disputants,* who *differ diametrically,* and have forgotten all *decency* in their *denunciations* and *declamatory* speeches, that all kinds of *divergent* and *dubious* tales are spread abroad. I held a *desultory discourse* yesterday with a *discriminating, discreet,* and *discerning* friend, who turns the whole affair into *derision.* He *denies* the reports which have been *disseminated,* and he has made a *declaratory* statement about them. He thinks it *derogatory* to his *dignity* to attempt the *discomfiture* of the *director's diabolical* enemies by other means; but I hope they will have their *desert.*

Diligent demolition is going on here. The *denizens* of Paris have constantly new *devices devised* for their *dwellings.* Some who *deprecate* all change *demur* and *descant* upon it as upon the *devastations* of a *deluge;* but the *diffusion* and *distribution* of employment cannot be *disadvantageous.* *Demagogues disseminate dissent* from the government; but the power of *democracy* is in *decadence,* and the present *dynasty* is not likely to be *disturbed* now, and will I think prove *durable.* The great *distress* and *disease* in consequence of the *drought* do not *decrease. Dysentery, diarrhœa, dyspepsia, diphtheria,* and *dropsy* are common in the *densely* peopled quarters. *Dispensaries* are *deemed* in*dispensable.* A doctor, whose *decease* has been a great loss, *dispensed decoctions* and *diminutive doses* or *drugs,* the strength of which was *diminished* by *diluents,* to aid the *di-*

gestion of the weak and *decrepid.* In *disparagement* of this plan, and to give *demonstrative disproof* of its *desirability,* some *declare* that it tends to the *detriment* of the sick, or to *debilitate* those who are already suffering from *debility.* *Decent* food is the great *desideratum ;* for *dough* of the most *deleterious* description is their chief *delicacy.*

Mr. ——, the great *distiller,* has met with public *disapprobation* from his *delinquencies* and *disabilities.* His *dividends* will be small. His young wife has done a good *deed* in *dispossessing* herself of her *diamonds.* My sister, who went to a *druggist's* this morning to buy *dentifrice* and *diachylon* plaster, met her there in *dishabille,* and with her hair *dishevelled,* — a great *desight.* She was *dolorous* and *dejected,* but said that no one could *dissuade* her from her purpose ; for her husband *dreaded dishonor* worse than the *depths* of a *dungeon :* but that, notwithstanding the *disparity* in their age, their *indissoluble* affection softened the *derision* of their *deceitful* foes. Nothing was *deducible* from the *dialogue,* except that he has *dissembled* the causes of his *downfall.*

I do not find much *difference* between Paris and London. Fashion is in both places the *deity* or *divinity* to whom *deference* is *deemed due.* A man, when *decoyed* into marriage with a *demure* and *dutiful daughter, devoted* to personal *decoration,* naturally *demands* a large *dowry.* This is *declared despicable.* The parents often wish the marriage to be *deferred,* and *displeasure* and *disquietude* are the result ; and *disinterestedness* is said to be a *delusion.*

The *debates* in the Assembly are *discussed* without *danger*; but the emperor's policy, though said to be *divulged*, cannot be *deciphered*. A *dignitary* of a southern *diocese* is in *disgrace* for *daring* to express his *detestation* of it, and to *decide* that it is *indefensible*. In other days, he might have been *decapitated* for thus *declaiming*. But it is in*disputable* that the emperor *dallies* both with Rome and Austria, whilst the *decree* which accepts the *declaration* of Italian in*dependence*, is *definitely decisive* as to the safety of the Italian *duchies*. The *delegates* at Turin are in a *delirium* of *delight*, and address him as their *deliverer*. The *demise* of the *decrepid* pope would *doubtless* solve the emperor's *dilemma*, and be followed by the *departure* from Rome of the French *dragoons*, who, though *dauntless* as *dragons*, must feel their *duties* to be *dreary drudgery*. They have *demeaned* themselves well. *Drunkenness* and *dram-drinking* have nearly *disappeared*, whilst they are *driven* to relieve their *dulness* by *ditties* and *drolleries*.

You know that I like to *dabble* in politics and art, though I do not *dogmatize* about them, but always speak with *diffidence*, and would no more pronounce *dogmatically* upon them, than upon a *doctrinal dogma*, such as the in*defectability* of the Church. There is a *deficiency* of artistic taste just now. *Dense* shadows and *dazzling* lights, without general *density* and *depth* of tone, are to be seen in the *daubs* placed in the shop *doorways*. I have *discovered* a *diptych*, painted by Giotto; and, after *deliberating* long, I

have given *discretionary* powers for its purchase.
It was painted for an Italian *ducal* family. The
last *descendant* is just *dead*. His property is *divided*
and *dispersed*, and the owner of the *diptych*, who is
dwarfed in intellect, and can scarcely *distinguish*
a *daffodil* from a *distaff*, has no more *distinctive*
ideas of art, than of the history of the *Decretals*, or
the meaning of *decemvirate*.

Distribute my regards to all my friends. I think
of you *daily*. Write to me *duly* every week. My
sister keeps a *diary*, so that we have a *diurnal*
record of the *divers* objects which we see, and the
diverse opinions which we form of them. The *dual*
number is very pleasant for travelling, though my
sister has rather *dronish* habits, and is inclined to
drowsiness and *dreaminess*. Once it was *different*:
then she rose at *dawn*, visited the *dairy*, and dis-
coursed by her *digits* with the *deaf* and *dumb dairy-*
maid. Strong as a *dromedary*, and fleet as a *doe* or
a *deer*, she rambled to a *distance* over the *dewy*
meadows, *dexterously* jumped over *deep ditches*, and
from *dizzy* heights, and came back in *disarray*.
She never needed to be *dieted*, and would have sung
a *dirge* of *despair*, if *denied* the *delight* of dancing
to her *dulcimer*. We *dubbed* her the *deity* of the
woods; and *dedicated* to her *doggerels* and *distichs*.
But since the *day* when she came home *dripping*
and half *dazed* after fishing for *dace* with the *Dean*
of *Derry*, and had such *difficulty* in *drying* herself,
she has *dismissed* the hope of health.

This seems a *digression*; but I *desired* to state,

that we found *Doctor* Green's *direction* in the *directory*, and went to him; but he is *undoubtedly* in his *dotage*, and unworthy of his *diploma*. He was *dressed* in a remarkable *doublet*, and talked *dribbling* nonsense; and I hear he is universally *decried*. He *devotes* himself to *dice*, and to *dramatic* amusements, so that he is in *debt*, and *duns* are for ever *dunning* him. It *demanded* some *dexterity*, and what may be *deemed* a *dodge*, to free ourselves from him. Your friend, Mr. *Deacon*, has *determinately* and *doggedly* taken up his *defence*, and has nearly fought a *duel* for him, though *duelling* is out of fashion. But he is a *devotee* to Dr. Green's plan, and in fact is called his *disciple*; though he understands it no more than he does the Hebrew of the Book of *Deuteronomy*. I hear also that Dr. Green is *divorced* from his wife, and is a *deist*, and that *deism* is on the increase; but some *deduction* must be made from common report. The *dial*-plate of my watch warns me to use *diligence*. I trust my letter may *dispel* your anxiety about me, and that some pleasure will be *derivable* from it. I am writing after *dessert*. When my plans have received their full *development*, you shall hear more. My letters are *diffuse* and *doleful*. I know my *dulness* increases: but I am no *dissembler*; and nothing, I feel, will *dissever* our affection. My *disbursements* are heavy, and make me wish I could hide in a *desert*. Adieu. Yours,

A. B.

P.S.— Is the borough of —— to be *disfranchised*?

and will the *dissenters* and other *dissidents* unite to oppose the ministry? Can your nephew obtain letters *dimissory*? Should *diæresis* be printed with a *diphthong*? Forgive these *discursive* questions. Good night, — I go to my *dormitory*. That *dunce, Daniel Dawson,* has sent me a *duplicate* copy of my uncle's *dissertation* on the *diameter* of the moon. If I could *deposit* it with any one here, I should leave it behind me. There are some curious remarks at the end, about the *deltas* made by great rivers when they *disembogue* through various mouths.

LETTER XII.

FROM A. B. TO C. D.

MARSEILLES, March, 1865.

My dearest Friend, — *Each epistle* that I receive from you makes me *eager* for more. I *earnestly exhort* you to be *equally energetic* with myself in keeping your *epistolary engagement.* You fear being *egotistical,* but I cannot too *emphatically express* my opinion that *everything* you say is *edifying.* After this *eulogistic exordium,* you will need no more *entreaties.*

We have had an *enchanting, easy,* and *expeditious* journey to Avignon, — a city of *excessive ecclesiastical* interest, having been *erewhile,* in a time of *emergency,* considered *eligible* as a residence for the popes, who *embellished* it *extremely.* My *equability* and *equanimity* were however *exhibited* most *exemplarily* in the *endurance* of the *extraordinary esca-*

pades of an *eccentric* courier, whose *eccentricities* have been *exasperating*, and have caused *endless embarrassments*. He *esteems* himself *entirely equal* to the *executive* department; and, *eschewing* my orders, *executes* his own. For *example:* we arrived at Dijon in the *evening*, in a state of *exhaustion*, having had no *edibles* for hours. On *entering* our apartment, my sister *exclaimed*, " Order *eggs!* " and I *echoed* the *exclamation*. They were *eatables easily* cooked, and also *economical*. The courier was *employed* on the *errand*, but no *eggs* came. The reason was not long *enigmatical*. My *emissary* had ordered an *elaborate entertainment*, as *expensive* as for an *emperor;* and when I *expostulated* and *exploded* in wrathful *epithets*, he stood *erect*, not offering *excuses*, or in any way *extenuating* his offence, but assuring me, that, although an *extemporaneous effort excogitated* by himself, *even* an *epicure* would be satisfied with the *elegant* result. My sister looked *emaciated:* her hunger was *excruciating*. But the courier, in *exulting exhilaration*, *exhorted* her to *endure*. *Eventually* the *eatables* appeared. The *effluvium* which they *emitted* was not *etherial;* but the courier, with *encomiastic, ecstatic*, and *exuberant* delight, set them on the table. Soup, of an *emerald* hue, and thick as an *electuary;* meat, coarse as *elephants'* flesh; boiled *endive*, with other *execrable esculents:* such was the food prepared in the *epicurean Elysium* of Dijon! The courier's *effrontery* was wonderful. *Elevating* his *eyebrows*, and *elongating* his mouth, he *ejaculated*, " Alas! the cook's knowledge of his art is *elementary*. He has cooked only for *English eleemosynary* institutions, and this is his first *essay* on a more *extended* and *expansive* scale. Let him be *exonerated* and *exculpated* from blame. Though his *emoluments* are not *enough* to keep him, he is *expeditious, enterprising*, and *estimable*, and will *eventually* be *efficient ;* and at the *expiration* of a few years will be *eminent* in his profession." In this *exigency*, my *excitement* was, I fear, unequivocally *evinced*. The courier made a speedy *exit* from the apartment, being *expelled* by *enforced evolutions*, which, however, were no *equivalent* or *expiation* for the *enormity* of his offence, though his *expulsion* plainly *expressed* my opinion of his conduct. My sister *entreated* for coffee, as an *emollient*, and said she would *eke* out her repast with bread and butter. Her *euphonious* voice shook, but the *evenness* of her *essentially* sweet disposition was undisturbed by my *ebullition*. I *embraced* her, and assured her that I was much *edified* by her *example ;* and I think my *endearments* soothed her. She *ensconced* herself in an *embrasure* of the window, seated herself on a stool placed *edgewise*, and took to her *embroidery* with an *evangelical* meekness quite *exemplary*. My *exasperated* feelings were not thus *ephemeral*, and the *equipoise* and *equilibrium* of my temper were not *easily* restored. An *equinoctial* gale could not indeed have been more tempestuous. No pope when *excommunicating* a king, and no king when *exiling* a subject, could have felt more indigant than I did both with cook and courier. An *exorbitant* bill, full of *errors* and *extortions*, was sent in to us the next morning. I declined paying more than could *equitably* be asked: this *engendered* another *earthquake*. With marked *emphasis*, I made an *extemporary exhortation* to the courier, and he *equivocated, exaggerated*, and *enunciated* lies. Yet, in spite of these *encroachments*, his *eligibility* for his post is, in some respects, so great, that I fear I should *err* in sending him away. He has been *especially educated* for it; and though his conduct is somewhat *equivocal*, and his folly is *egregious*, he is no *eavesdropper*. The *exactitude* of his accounts, and his *exertions* to *extricate* us in *extremities, extinguish* my ire, and *enable* me even sometimes to *extol* him. If I were to discover *embezzlement*, it would *effectually* settle the matter.

From Dijon we went to Lyons, the *emporium* of trade, and *esteemed* the second city in France. My sister purchased some *enamelled ear-rings* there, and also a little carved *easel*, whilst, after visiting a dentist and having a tooth *extracted*, I called on an *engineer*, and saw some new steam-*engines*. He is a man of *erudition*, and we talked much of *electricity* and the *electric* telegraph. I also visited a famous *empiric*, who thinks he has discovered an *efficacious* cure for all diseases, from *erysipelas* to *elephantiasis*. It is a kind of *emetic;* but its ingredients are an *enigma*, and their *efficacy* is doubted. I hear there are *enchanting excursions* in the *environs* of Avignon; but our day of *embarcation* is fixed, as we must be at Rome before *Easter:* we ought to have been there soon after the *Epiphany*. If you can send me, by *Edward Ellison*, the *eleventh edition* of *Elegiac* poems, and *Edmonstone's* translation of the *Eclogues* of Virgil, said to be the best *extant*, with *Evans's English Etymology*, it will *enliven* me. I should like an *Encyclopedia* and Aristotle's *Ethics*, but it would *entail* too much expense. My sister, who is recovering her naturally *elastic* spirits, and is full of *enthusiasm* for study, wants her copy of Gray's *Elegy* with the *elegant embossed* binding, some lace *edging*, her *ermine* boa, and the *epigrammatic* verses by Miss *Ewart*, who certainly is an *embryo* poetess. They are in her *escritoire*.

Is it true that there is an *estrangement* between the *editor* of the " Times " and his *epistolary* correspondent in America? and that the *emendations* and *erasures* made by the former in the *erudite* compositions of the latter is the cause? I have been reading an *epic* poem by *Edmund Evelyn*. The *episodes*, though *extraneous* to the purpose of the poem, and sometimes requiring an *exposition*, are *exceedingly exciting* and *effective*. He *emulates* men of *effulgent* genius; but the *emanations* from his pen have as yet met with no *encouragement;* and I am told that he is *envied* by many *enemies*, and therefore intends to *emigrate.*

The length of this letter is scarcely *excusable*, so farewell. Yours *ever*,   A. B.

LETTER XIII.

FROM C. D. TO A. B.

LONDON, March, 1865.

My dear Friend, — I have written *eight epistles*, — at least, this is the *eighth*. I am *encompassed* by papers, which I must *indorse*, and I must then correct some *erroneous* accounts, together with a list of *errata* for an *expurgated edition* of the *English Essayists*, from which every objectionable passage has been *eliminated* and *expunged*; and afterwards make an *effort* to write an *explanation* of the *equator*, the *ecliptic*, the *equinoxes*, and the *elliptical* orbits of comets.

If I am *e'er* again *exempted* from overwork and *excitement*, I shall be *enchanted*. My *eye*-sight is suffering. I sometimes think that, at the *expiration* of this month (if I do not *expire* before), I shall *e'en* take your *encouraging* advice, and *experimentally* test the *efficacy* of the watery *element* to re-*establish elasticity* of mind and body; in other words, I shall try sea-bathing. *Equestrian exercise* is *expensive*, and I have no *equipage*, so that I feel *entombed* in London. I shall try to find lodgings on the *Esplanade* at ———, where several new houses have been *erected*. It will be an *epoch* in my *existence* when I *emerge* from this great town, in which *every* one is *engrossed* with his own affairs, and find myself watching the *ebb* and flow of the tide, and the *eddies* of the *estuary* at the mouth of the Thames. It will be to me like the *Elysian* fields, or a draught of the *elixir* of life.

The *Earl* of *Exeter*, who was upon the *eve* of his *espousals*, has died suddenly. His sister, whom we used to liken to an *eagle* on his *eyry*, is his *executrix*. The *eligibleness* or *eligibility* of this choice is doubtful. *Every one* was in *expectancy* that there would be *executors* also; but the earl was especially fond of his sister, who is an *enticing enchantress*. It will, I fear, be an *exemplification* of the *evils* of *exclusiveness;* for the relations are likely to be *eternally* at *enmity*, though the property is *equably* and *equitably* divided. The *estates* of the *earldom* were *erst* immense, but a large portion *escheated* to the Crown at the *era* when the *Electorial* House of Hanover were *elected* to fill the *English* throne. The family *exchequer* is, however, well filled. The race, once not only *extrinsically* great, but also *ennobled* by talent, has become *effete*, and is nearly extinct. The late earl was like an *enervated exotic*. His *effeminacy* was proverbial, though he was a man of *erudition endued* with some talent. His *elocution* was *excellent*, and I have heard his *etchings* highly *extolled*. He was an *excessive eater :* some say he died from *eating eels*. I know myself, that he was subject to *epilepsy*, and had *erewhile* an *excrescence* which required *excision*. There was also a tendency to an *eruption* on his face, which could not be *eradicated*, though several *embrocations* were tried; and he had a cough at times, with a good deal of *expectoration*. Marks of the *extrusion* of

extravasated blood were found on him.   The rumor
of an *epidemic* fever or an *endemic* complaint has
arisen, but it is too *extravagant* to be believed.
His *emblazoned escutcheon* is placed over the door-
way of his *empty* house, which looks as if *efts* and
emmets inhabited it, and would never again be *extir-
pated* or *exterminated*.   No one who sees it, can be
an *envier* of the *exaltation* or *elevation* of another;
for, as it is said in his *epitaph*, " death *equalizes* fortune, and brings all men to an *equality*."

Our *enrolment* for volunteers continues: I am
myself an *ensign*.   I have not *examined* the *edicts*
which have been set forth, and the laws which have
been *enacted* upon the subject, but nothing but good
can *ensue* from the movement.

Tell me about the *excavations* at Rome, and
whether the *effigies* of two cardinals have been
burnt, and what is the value of the statue lately
found there; also, whether the French are likely to
evacuate the city.   They can never be *ejected* by
force; but an *embassy* from the Italian government
might lead to some *equitable* arrangement, and herald
their *egress*.   I will gladly be the *executor* of your
wishes, but I shall need more *explicit explications*.

My niece, who searched your sister's *escritoire*,
found, in one of the *enclosures*, an *emery* cushion, and
a faded branch of *eglantine* which still *exhaled* some
perfume; a packet of *envelopes;* an *exquisite* sketch
of a *ewe*-lamb; a piece of silk about an *ell* wide, the
color of *emerald* green; a copy of the *epilogue* to
some play; a description of the Jewish *Ephod,* and

of the *emblems* of the four *Evangelists ;* a history of *exorcists* and *exorcism ;* a sonnet on the *expanse* of the *empyreal* heavens ; and an *epitome* of the means by which it was once *endeavored* to foretell *events* from the *entrails* of beasts. My niece made an *ejaculatory* comment after this *enumeration,* and *exclaimed,* " Is this *emblematical* of the contents of the brain ? " Adieu. Yours, &c. c. d.

P.S. — I was asked the other day by one of the Queen's *equerries,* who, though as stiff as an *espalier-*tree, was *evidently* as *erratic* in his mind as a knight-*errant,* to *explain* the meaning of *eclecticism, exegesis, exegetical, epithalamium* and *euthanasia ;* to define *entity ;* to distinguish between *elicit* and illicit ; to give an *example* of *elision ;* and to describe the form used when a jury is *empannelled.* Have you carried away my copy of the Bishop of Oxford's *Eucharistica ?* also, do you agree with *Everett's* book on *Ethnology ?*

LETTER XIV.

FROM A. B. TO C. D.

Civita Vecchia, March, 1865.

My dear *Friend,* — The now *formidable fortifications* of Civita Vecchia show that we have *finally* parted from that *infelicitous* sea, the Mediterranean. I say, un*feignedly,* may I never be *fated* to re-cross it ! Our *fatigue* is great ; for it was *frightfully* rough : much rougher than it was on that *fourth* of *February,* when we were nearly lost in the *Frith* of *Forth.* The wind rose in *fitful* gusts, and soon the *fretted* waves tossed *furiously*, and their *furrows* — deep as *fissures*, and *frothed* and *freckled* with *fantastic feathery flakes* of *foam* — made our hearts *flutter* and *fluctuate* between *fear* and hope. Our vessel was as large as a *frigate*, and seemed to *fly* through the *fathomless* water, as *flies* pass through the air. If we had been *fleeing* from an enemy, we might have been *fearless ;* but though I am *familiarized* to danger by the *frequency* of my voyages, I esteem it *folly* to *face* it unnecessarily.

The *freezing frigidity* of the weather, the *fuliginous fumes* with which our room is *fumigated* from an adjacent *flue,* the *flimsy furniture,* and the *frugal* provision of *fagots* for *fuel,* with which we are *favored,* increase the *forlornness* of this place. We thought to *forego flannel* in Italy, but we are *forced* to take to it, and even a *fustian* jacket would be comfortable to my *feelings.* The most *fastidious, finical,* and *fashionable,* however, would not *find* the *food faulty. Famished folk* though we are, we shall not die of *famine,* when we have a *fillet* of beef, delicate as the *flesh* of *fowls ;* a *fricasse fitted* for a *festival,* together with a *fritter,* made with good *flour ;* some *fine filberts ;* and specimens of the *finny* tribe, which, though rather *flaccid* and *flabby,* are *fresher* than can be had at a London *fishmonger's* shop.

My sister is *forbidden* to eat *fruit,* or *farinaceous food ;* but if it were not so, the *fruitage* of the season would be *fruitlessly* sought for. *Fruiterers'* shops are, of course, unknown. The *fertility* and *fecundity* of the *fertile* Campagna will no doubt *fulfil* my expectations by and by, but it has not *fulfilled* them yet. I hear of *fountains* and *festoons* of vines near Rome, but the land round Civita Vecchia often lies *fallow*. In the *fuss* of departure, a *flagon* of good wine was *forgotten* by us. My sister has made *futile* attempts to drink the *filmy fluid* which is given us here; but she leaves me to *finish* the *flask*, for she *fancies* it has a disagreeable *flavor*. I can imagine that, in *feverish* cases, when a *febrifuge* is needed, it might be *feasible* to mix it with *filtered* water.

I *flattered* myself that I should escape the *fallibility* and *falsity* of public reports when I came abroad; but this was a *fallacious fantasy*. The countries in which *freedom* is unknown are often the *focus* of *falsehood*. *Fictitious* tales are *fabricated*, and *foisted* into newspapers; the *frenzy* of the *froward, fickle,* and *frivolous* is *fostered* by them, and the success of the good cause is *fatally frustrated*. For instance: in the late battle, General *F*——, who is said to hold the doctrines of *fatalism*, seems to have been *fundamentally* at *fault*. His conduct is declared to have been *foully flagitious*. A *fierce feud* has broken out between him and the colonel of a regiment of *fusileers*, respecting the *fusee* of a gun, and threats have been *fulminated* against him, which, however, he receives as mere *formalities*. This is but a *fractional* portion of the *furago* of new-*fangled* lies which I have heard. People seem to cast *furtive* glances at the *future*, and would *fain forestall* it, *forgetting* that they are but *finite*.

Fighting goes on at the *frontiers*, but only with the *framentary* but un*flagging* bands of *felons* and *fugitives*, who are *flitting* about, and will never hoist the *flag* of truce, or *forego* a meeting with a foe. They *frequent fenny* swamps and *forests*; under the *foliage* of the latter, they march, carrying *phials* of brandy, and *forage* for their horses. They cross *ferries* and *fordable* rivers, and are clever in *finesse* and *feints*; and, being *familiar* with the country, require no *flashing flambeaux*, but only the stars of the *firmament*, to light them in their night marches. According to the *fore-cited* tales, there seems to be a *fatality* in the *feebleness* of the troops sent against them, and who too *frequently fraternize* with them; whilst un*fortunately, fortuitous* events have *furthered* their plans.

It is said that the government is *financially* weak; that *fraudulent forgeries, felonies,* and the *failures* and *filchings* of high *functionaries,* have *fleeced* the revenue and *fiscal* department. The *financier*, who made so many *fallacious* promises, has, I am told, *forfeited* all claim to confidence, and, in *fact*, is considered *fatuous*; but I have not *fastened* my *faith* upon these *fugatious* reports, and *fully* believe that the roving bands will be *ferreted* out and put to *flight*, and then the *festering* sore which is so *fraught* with in*felicity* to the *fabric* of society will be healed.

I ask your *forgiveness* for this *figurative* expres-

sion. I am not given to *facetiæ* or *facetious* stories,
or to *flourishing* and *florid* tales of *funny* and *farcical* adventures ; otherwise, I could amuse you with
the *feminine fopperies* of our male *friends*, the
freaks and *fretfulness* of some of our *flippant, flashy,
female fellow*-travellers, who, *flittering* away their
time, *flit* about like *fairies*, bent on *fascinating* by
frolics and *finery* and *frippery furbelows*. The un-
faltering friendship of one man has, however, imbued
me with equal *friendliness*. His *forefathers* were
fullers, but his *father* owned an iron *foundry ;* and
he knows a great deal about the *friction* and *frangi-
bility* of *ferruginous* material, especially iron *filings*.
He has made a collection of *fossils*, has a *faculty* for
music, and plays with *facility* on the *flageolet*, and
has composed a *fugue*.

I talk to him about *forensic* eloquence, and we
discuss the *feudal* times, *feods, feoffs,* or *fiefs,* and the
feudatory remains of the present day. He is in-
flexibly of opinion that a *federal* union is un*fitting*
for Italy. He is no *fanatic*, but the *fervency* and
fixity of his opinions, and the *forcible fluency* of his
language, are remarkable, though he is very *forbear-
ing*. He is indeed as *firm* as a *first*-rate *fencer*,
rigid as a line drawn by a schoolmaster's *ferule* or
ferula, and severe as a lictor with his *fasces*. His
features are not *fine*, and are rather *flattened*, with
the exception of his *forehead*.

My sister looks *forward* to the *fragrance* of the
flowery treasures of the Campagna ; she talks of
examining *filaments* and *fibers, fungus* and *fungi*,

and all kinds of *fungous* wonders. I do not wish to *fidget* her by throwing a doubt on the *fruition* of her hopes, but I cannot but *feel* their *futility*. I believe that, in Italy, the *fervid* heat of the sun in all its *fulgency* is as much *feared* as a source of *febrile* complaints, and is as often a cause of *funerals* and *funereal* ceremonies, as the *feculent* moisture of *falling* leaves in England; and the *frailness* of my sister's constitution *fills* me with the dread of her *fading* entirely. Write to me on the *fifth* and *fifteenth* of the month. I saw but *few friars* in *France*, where there are not the *fiftieth* part of the number to be *found* in Italy. *Fleas* abound, and *flee* swiftly, as they do elsewhere.

I see that *Fortescue's foolish* book, entitled "*Filial* Duty not a *Fantasm*," is published with a splendid *frontispiece*. The *first* page, with an account of *falchions* and *faldstools*, *frightened* me from *further* progress. I would much sooner study a *folio* copy of the *Fathers*. My friend *Fawcet* has written to me from *Florence*, about a young *foal*, and the *foggy* weather, but I would rather hear about religious *formularies*, *Florentine* paintings, and *frescos*.

My sister looks at me *frowningly*, and warns me that letter-writing must be but a *fleeting* pleasure, and I *formally* take my leave, and say *farewell*. Yours ever,   A. B.

P.S. — We find *fees* required here as in England. My sister is just learning the difference between a *French franc* and an English *florin*. *Fancy* the ignorance of *Frank Fitzgerald*, who, in writing, does not know how to distinguish between *faun*, a satyr, and *fawn*, a young deer. He will confuse *Francis*, his own name, and *Frances*, his sister's name, next!

LETTER XV.

FROM C. D. TO A. B.

MARGATE, March, 1865.

My dear Friend,—I sent you a *gossipping graphic* private letter, and you notice it no more than a public *gazette!* Surely you are a *greedy gudgeon*, and are un*grateful* and *grumbling*. My last *greeting* was a *gratuitous gift;* and yet you *groan* and *growl*, and instead of *giving gracious* and *gentle* thanks, like a *genteel* and *genial gentleman*, you behave like a *genuine Gentile*.

Words may *glide glibly* from the *gifted* pen of a *genius;* I am not one of that *galaxy*, but belong to the *generality* of mankind who may be *generically grouped* together as *geese*.

I cannot *gabble* about *gravitation, geological* discoveries, the *Georgics*, and the *Gnostic* heresy. I cannot talk of *gradients*, and the *gibbosity* of the *gibbous* moon. I have never *gloated* over the statues of the *gigantic Gorgon* and the dying *Gladiator*, though I do know the derivation of *gymnastics*, the use of a *gymnasium*, and the meaning of *graniverous* and *graminivorous*. But my own knowledge is like *gossamer's gauze*, or *goldbeater's* skin, *glistening* and *glittering*, but *gone* as soon as touched, *Girlish gar-*

9

rulity is all you will *get* from me now. I am at the sea. I do not know who is to be *generalissimo* of the Italian army, or *governor* of Florence, and can give no opinion as to the *government* of the Italian kingdom, but I certainly would not *guarantee* its continuance.

I have not read *Godfrey's* " Commentary on the Book of *Genesis*," or " *Gleanings* and *Gropings*," by an Oxford *Graduate ;* neither shall I study *Greenwood's* new *German Grammar*, and his *general* rules for the *genitive* case. I have given up *gravity*, and am now *guardian* to my little *god-daughter Gertrude*, and her brother *George*, who are staying with me. They are the children of *Georgiana Griffiths*, old Mrs. *Graham's grand-daughter*. You would scarcely *guess* that we are now all watching a *grinning grimalkin* on the wall. *Grizzled*, even *gray* though I am, the *gaiety* of these *guileless* little *gypsies* fills me with *glee*. Their *glances*, *grimaces*, *giggling*, and *gesticulations* chase away *gloom*. There is no *gall* in their nature, and they have never known *grief*. I cannot indeed understand *grieving* when with them.

We have laid aside the *Gazetteer* and the *geographical* maps to study the *geography* of nature. Grammar and *grammatical* speech are forgotten. The *genealogies* and *genealogical* lists of kings are never repeated. We make *grottos* in the rocks, drink *ginger*-beer, and help a *gawky* boy called *Jem* to find *gems* amongst the pebbles. A *garrison* being near, we have men *galloping gaily* about in *gorgeous gorgets* and *gaudy gear.* The children *gaze* on them with *great* delight.

Yesterday, we were near the *glacis* of a fortification, and were watching a dog *gnawing* a bone, when a *group* of *grenadiers* came up, and the *girths* of a horse *getting* slack, the rider *got* off. The animal wished to *graze,* and began *gambolling* near the *gable*-ended house which is said to be frequented by *gamblers.* His *gyrations* filled the little *girl* with *groundless* fears. *Guessing* her fright, the soldier made a *gesture* to calm her; but she fled as from a *ghost,* and, being without *guidance, grew* more alarmed, and fell at length, *grovelling* on the *gravelly* path. She was in a *grotesque guise,* begrimed as by a *gridiron* on a kitchen *grate,* when she came in; but she *gloried* in her adventure, and *gave* a *gasconading* account, which made us as *gay* as *grigs* all the evening.

Our boats are not *graceful gondolas,* neither do the men row as *gracefully* as *gondoliers;* but we are far *gayer* than the *grander* people who *glidingly* float upon the *glassy* waters of Venice. I am full of *gratitude* for this rest, and do not *grudge* or look *grudgingly* upon the *gaieties* of others. The *gnarled* oaks in the *glassy glades* shelter us from the *glare* of the *glaring* sun. The children like *gardening,* and delight in watching the *gardener grafting* buds: they give the *groundsel* to their birds, and *gather* for me *gilly*-flowers, *guelder* roses, and *gentians* from their little *garden.* If our *giblet* soup is made up of rather *gelatinous gizzard;* if the *griskin* broiled on the gridiron is *gristly;* and if the *greasiness* of the *grilled goose* dressed with *greasy gravy,* and flavored with *garlic,* is not very tempting,—yet I can fall back upon *grist* and *gruel;* and the children, if allowed to *gormandize,* will eat almost any thing *greedily.* This afternoon we shall go to see a *grampus* which has been caught.   The children are more *gregarious* than I am.   A *governess* and her pupils who live near are *going* with us.   You know I never liked *gadding* about, and, except when I am *gouty,* can sleep well in a *garret,* or even in a *granary.*

I have had a *glimpse* of your cousin *Geoffrey,* who is at The *Grange.*   He intends to be a good *geometrician,* and is deep in *geometrical* studies. He also hopes to be a *Grecian* scholar, and is *grappling* with the *Greek grammarians,* and tells me he thinks he has a *glimmering* as to their meaning, and finds the *gerunds* easy.   He talked *grandiloquently,* and says his *guerdon* for his present labors will be a journey to the Swiss *glaciers,* where he intends to study the various *glacial* theories.

The *glazier* is just come to mend the window, which was broken by a *graceless* servant-girl, who threw a *goblet* at a *gobbling, gluttonous* turkey-cock. It has been un*glazed* for two days; but we found some *glutinous gum* in a *gallipot,* with which we *gummed* and *glued* paper over the hole.

Pray do not let the *gibbering* of foreign *gibberish gradually* corrupt your taste, and especially avoid *gallicisms.*   No language is like that of *Greece;* and Italian, though *guiltless* of *gutturals,* is, **when** compared with it, like *gilder's gilt* when compared with *gold*. You will say this is a *gratuitous* insult to your favorite language.

Young *Guy*, the *grandson* of the chief member of the *Goldsmiths' guild*, has been accused of stabbing a *gunner*, who was standing on the *gunwale* of his vessel, whilst the sailors were practising *gunnery*. The man died of *gangrene*; but, as *Guy's guilt* was clear, *gyves* were put upon him, in spite of his *gentility*, and he has been sent to *gaol*. Some say that he had drunk several *gills* of *gin*, and was willing to throw down the *gauntlet* to any one; and others, that he was *goaded* on by the *gibes* of two boys, sons of a spirit-*gauger* and a *glover*. However that may be, he has *grieved* his mother, and caused her a fit of *giddiness*, ending in a *gastric* fever. Though the worst was *glozed* over to her, yet the *ghastliness* of her *ghost*-like face, when she heard the fact, I shall never forget. Her son was a *gallant* fellow, who *gave* way to none of the *grosser* vices, though he would *gnash* his teeth when angry. He was un-*gallant* in his manner to ladies, and always hated *gewgaws*. Some say his disposition was *griping* and *grasping*, but I doubt it.

The children have been eating some *guava* jelly and *gelatine* lozenges bought at the *grocer's*, and are now *going* to draw me pictures of *goggle*-eyed *giants*, *gigantic goblins*, *goatherds* and *goddesses*, with *gabardines* of a bright *gamboge* color, *garnished* with *green girdles*, *gauntlets* on their hands, *garlands* on their heads, and *greaves* upon their legs. In return,

I am to give them a picture of a *grazier* hanging on a *gibbet ;* but an organ-*grinder* and a boy with a kind of *guitar* have just come up, and now the little ones are both dancing *giddily,* — moving as quickly as *gnats,* or creatures of the *genus grasshopper.* I sometimes think they have taken a *gallon* of laughing-*gas.*

You will see nothing so *gay* in Italian *galleries,* and nothing so pretty as their *glossy* hair. *Groats* and *guineas,* and even the riches of Spanish *galleons,* are nothing to me now that I have reached my *goal,* and am with them by the sea-side. I never speak *gruffly ;* and am *garrulous* with the nurse about *gowns* and the *garniture* of dresses, *galloon* and *gloves ;* and I also administer *globules,* and give medical advice *gratis.* The blossom of a *gherkin,* which is *germinating* in the garden, reminds me of the *granulated* fruits of the South. Are they not *glorious ?* Do you know whether *guano* is ever used in Italian farming? Can you understand the *genuflexions* in the Roman-Catholic service? Did you take the *Glossary* of Architecture with you? Tell me if you ever meet with any *glosses* of ancient writers. Ever yours,   C. D.

LETTER XVI.

FROM A. B. TO C. D.

ROME, March, 1865.

My dear Friend, — You will be glad to *hear,* that I have *here* at last found *halcyon* days ; and that the *harass* of England seems as far away as the era of the *Hegira*, or the time of the *Heptarchy*. *Heigho!* *how has* it *happened* that I never *hastened* to Rome before, though I have *hankered* after it *half* my life! *Henceforth* I shall look forward *hopefully* to the winter, if I can spend it in Rome. My *home* is on a *height*, not so *high* as the Pincian *Hill*, but *happily higher* than the Piazza, which is *haunted* by those who like *hubbub* and *hurly-burly*. Rome is a *historical hodgepodge*. *Handsome* and *habitable houses*, *hospitals*, *hostelries*, *heathen* temples, —— once polluted by *hecatombs*, but now *hallowed* by *hosannas* and *hallelujahs*, —— all *hedged* and *hemmed* in by *hideous hovels*, form a *heterogeneous* picture, as difficult to describe as the position of the *hierarchical* power which now *holds* the *helm* of government.

Whether this *hierarchy* will be able to stand, is as puzzling as the *hieroglyphics* of Egypt. Censures are *hurled* against *heretical* books and *heterodox* opinions, which are considered *heinous* offences; but *heresy* and *heretics* are *harbored* in the city, and though there may be no great *heresiarch* to whom all will *hearken*, yet the *humor* of the people is not what it was *heretofore;* and they will not take *heed* to *harangues* to which they are *habituated*, though they are too *helpless* to break out into open *hostility*.

I *hired* a *hackney* yesterday, and rode with a party, one of whom was a *handsome* lady in the *habit* of a *huntress*, across the Campagna. The *herbage* was lovely, and a *herbalist* would no doubt have found treasures for his *herbal;* but my *hilarious* friends cared for them no more than for *hemlock* and *henbane*. They rode *helter*-shelter, making *hazardous* leaps, which disturbed *herdsmen* and *herds* of *heifers ;* besides committing great *havoc* amongst the *herbaceous* fields, to the *hindrance* of the *hirsute hirelings*, who were *hoeing* there, and who evidently thought they were *hippogriffs* or *hobgoblins*.

At length a *harrow, hidden* by some *hurdles* and a *hedge*, made a lady's *horse* fall back on its *haunches*. The *heedless* rider, who is somewhat of a *hoyden*, was thrown *heavily*, and her *habiliments* caught in the *hinge* of a gate. The *hindermost horseman* coming to her *help* floundered in a *humid* ditch, and, but for an *honest hoary hedger* who was about to *hew* some wood, but was *hailed* by some of the party, and *hobbling* up *helped* both, the *hilarity* of the expedition might have been at an end. The lady *hopped* about, and *halted* on one foot, and every one kept on *hoping* she was not *hurt ;* but she really had not even a *headache*, though she was *hugely* offended, and behaved very *haughtily*, because some one talked *humorously* to her, and gave her a *hortatory homily* against riding *hap-hazard* over *hillocks*.

She is an *heiress*, who desires to be a *heroine*, and who, instead of considering her fall a *humiliation*, thinks that she behaved *heroically*. The gentleman who was with her, and who is the son of a great *historian* or *horticulturist*, I forgot which, thinks she has a *hectic* flush, and that her *health* will suffer. At parting, he gave her a nosegay of *hyacinths*, *heartsease*, *harebells*, and *heliotrope*, and, *heaving* a sigh, *hoped* she would accept his *homage* for her *heroism.*   Unless he is a *hypocrite,* I should say that his *heart* was touched, and that he wishes her to add to his *happiness* by allowing him to lead her to the *hymeneal* altar.   Pray do not confound this with *halter.*

My sister is gone out to buy *holland* and *huckaback,* or something required for *housewifery.*   She tells me, that the way she is forced to *higgle* and *haggle* about prices almost sends her into *hysterics.* We have a *hospitable, harmless* neighbor : he plays on the *hautboy* and the *harpsichord,* and sings *Handel* in a *harsh* voice, till he is *hoarse.*   But he *handles* him unmercifully, and produces most *horrible* and in*harmonious hissing* and *humming* sounds.   He is devoted to the *histrionic* art, and is a student of *heraldry ;* and has a *halberd,* a *hauberk,* a *harquebuse* (or, as I believe it is often written, arquebuse), and a *habergeon, hanging* on his walls.   He is besides very *hypochondriacal,* and is always talking of *homœopathy* and *hydropathy,* except when he discourses upon the *hallucinations* of *hagiographers.*

His name is *Hugh Harrison :* he is a *haggard* looking man, scarcely *human* in his appearance, for he has a *hairy* face of a dark *hue,* and always makes me think of a *hedgehog.*   He dresses like a *harlequin :* his language is full of *hyperbole,* and if he writes a note, it is not simply, but *hyperbolically ;* and he delights also in arguing upon an *hypothesis.* But I prefer certainties to *hypotheses,* and therefore, whenever he says, " speaking *hypothetically,*" I stop

him with all the *hard* words I can *heap* together,
and talk of *hydraulics* and *hydrostatics*, *hexameter*
verses, *hexagonal* and *heptagonal* buildings, and
horizontal lines.   I ask him if he ever saw a *hy-
grometer*, and if he can explain the meaning of
hypostasis and *hierophant ;* and I beg to know if a
hereditament is a *hereditary* and *heritable habitation.*

He must often long for a fit of *hiccough* to bring
me to a pause, or that my mouth should be *hermeti-
cally* sealed ; but he is a *humane* fellow, and we
hobble along together comfortably.   He has ordered
a *hogshead* of wine for me, red as *hippocras*, good
honey and fresh *herrings ;* and, if he is rather *hoggish*
in his *habits*, I am not *hypercritical.*   I cannot,
indeed, be a *hypocrite*, and *hypocritically* reward him
with *honied* words ; but I can and do *honor* him.   I
forgot to say, that he has a *hatred* of dogs, and a
horror of *hydrophobia.*   I believe he was born in
the other *hemisphere.*   His father was either a *hat-
ter*, a *haberdasher*, or a seller of *hardware.*   He had
not a *halfpenny* of his own when he began life, and
learnt no *handicraft*, though he was always *hammer-
ing* in a yard with a carpenter's *hammer*, and this
much *heightens* the strangeness of his knowledge.
He lives like a *hermit* in his *hermitage :* he is a very
good *Hebraist ;* many difficult *hebraisms* have been
explained by him.

I must tell you that your *handwriting* is not to be
read : some letters are *huddled* together, and then
there follows a *hiatus.*   I am glad you are at the
headland, and are *heedful* of your *health*, and have

healthful air. I thought you would have *hied* to the *hilly Highlands*, and fancied you watching the *hawk* in the air, and the *heron* by the lake, if not *hunting* the *hart* with *howling hounds*, and *hearkening* to the *halloos* and *huzzas* of *huntsmen;* but it would have been too *heating* in this season, which, though *heavenly*, is apt to make one *headachy*. My sister has bought a *hoop*-ring for your cousin, and a *handkerchief* which will be a good *head*-dress for your aunt: she has cut it in *halves*, and will send the *half* to you a few days *hence*, by a man going to England, a *hanger*-on of the Duke of *Hamilton*. He is a kind of *henchman*, whose grandfather, they say, was a *headsman*.

I do wish Roman shoemakers understood *heeling* and *heel*-piecing; but they are very *hazy* in their ideas, and extremely *heady*, going off in a *huff* when they are found fault with: yet they know no more of this part of their trade than they do of *houghing horses*.

I see that the Americans of the North have *hoisted* the national flag. Some have stated that the Republic has as many *heads* as a *hydra*. I *humbly hope*, *however*, that it will soon prove itself *homogeneous*, and that its wounds will be *healed*. Do tell me if there is now a *hippopotamus*, as well as a *hyena*, in the Zoological Gardens ; also, did your cousin *Henry*, who belonged to the *Hussars* die of *hemorrhage*, and who followed his *hearse?*

I have had some arguments with my sister, all *hinging* upon these points. We have *hugged* ourselves many times at being safely *housed* at **Rome,** and *having* no longer to cross that *horridly* stormy Mediterranean. Your *housekeeper* once asked me, if people kneel on *hassocks*, and use *hymnals*, in the Roman churches. Did she think these were signs of *holiness*, and that a service would be more *holily* conducted with than without them? They do sing *hymns*, I know. Now, good-bye. Yours ever,

A. B.

P.S. — My sister asks : Does *hyssop* grow in your part of England ? I wonder what the weather is like in your *hyperborean* regions. Here we have all the *harbingers* of summer.

LETTER XVII.

FROM C. D. TO A. B.

MARGATE, March, 1865.

My dear Friend, — I *imagined* that I should *inevitably* receive either an account of the *incidents* of some pleasant *jaunt*, or have the *infliction* of an *inordinately* long, though probably *ingenious* essay, on the *infallibility* of the Pope ; and you *indulge* me, *instead*, with a subject which is *incontestably* *infinitely* less *irksome* to yourself, — the *idiosyncrasies* of the *jolly*, and, as it would seem, somewhat *jovial*, *inhabitant* of your house. Your account of the *individual* is *inimitable*. It is so *indefinite*, that I have no *idea* whether he is a *Jew* or an *idiot*. He certainly is not *illiterate*, but he seems to reason very

illogically: and if it were not *illiberal* in me to give
an *immature judgment* upon a topic on which I am
immeasurably ignorant, I should say that he is *indu-
bitably incomparably inferior* to yourself; and that
the *incompatibility* of your tastes, and the *inanity*
and *insipidity,* I may almost say the *imbecility,* of
his character, must render your *juxta*-position at
this *juncture inopportune,* and your *intimacy inau-
spicious.* He appears to be *imperturbable,* and is
not likely, I suppose, to commit any *inadventencies;*
but your *impetuosity,* my dear friend, and the *incon-
siderateness inherent* in your *ingenuous* nature, often
induce you to do *incredibly indiscreet* things. In
fact, this friendship is *incongruous.* *Jaded* as I am,
and *immersed* in the *intricacies* of business, I still
seize an *interval* to write to you. I am not *jealous,*
and have no *intention* of *jeering,* but the *injudicious-
ness* of your conduct is *indefensible,* and must put you
in *jeopardy.* I entreat you to *institute inquiries* into
the history of this *individual,* whom I must call an
incognito. He may be an *idolater,* an *incendiary,* a
Jacobin, a *jackanape,* or *insolvent.* He may be covered with *ignominy.* His birth is *ignoble,* it may be
illegitimate. His hands may be *imbrued* with blood.
But, notwithstanding this *incertitude,* because he is
not an *ignoramus,* you deem his *innocency immacu-
late,* and look upon him as *imbued* with the highest
virtues. Your *immediate intention* in visiting Rome
was to collect *information* upon an *infinitude* of
interesting subjects; but you will become an *incor-
rigible irreclaimable idler,* under the *influence* of this

man, for you will have no *incentive* to exertion ; indeed, such companionship is *irreconcilable* with it.

I know how *insidiously* he will work upon one whose *instinctive intuitions* as to character are not quick, and who is therefore so open to *illusion* and *illusory imaginations* as yourself. *Insensibly*, and by *indiscernible* steps, you will become *inseparable* and *indivisible*, and will *involve* yourself *inextricably* in his affairs. Such is always your *impulse*. He will then *ingratiate* himself into your favor, and, by *inuendos* and *insinuations*, *incite* you to make *invidious* comparisons between himself and me, and the *irreparable injury* will be done. The bond which I *imagined indestructible*, *indissoluble*, and *inviolable*, will be broken, and *instead* of an *inalienable* and *immutable* affection, I shall be treated with an *inconstancy* which will render me *inconsolable*, for you have hitherto been *indispensable* to my happiness.

This is no *imaginary* or *ideal* case. I am not *infuriated* by *jealousy*, or *imagining impossibilities*. You may *ignore* what I say as to the *inexpediency* of this *inconceivably inane intimacy ;* but the fact is *incontrovertible*. Any person of *impartial judgment*, or who only wished to *judge* with *impartiality*, would *infallibly* see the *insanity* of *incurring* the risk which must result from *joining* yourself *intimately* with a person who may be not only guilty of *innumerable irrationalities* and *irregularities*, such as *infidelity* and *intemperance*, but the *iniquity*, *illegality*, and *indecency* of whose *illicit* proceedings may render him *infamous*. Are you sure that *intoxication* or, as some would say, *inebriety*, may not be laid to his charge?

But by this time my words may be *inefficacious* and *immaterial;* and you will listen to me with *incredulity*, and wish to assert your *independence*. The *intellectual* gifts of your new friend may have so *impressed* you, that all I can say will be *ineffectual*. *Impressible* as you are, and tempted to *idolize* persons *intrinsically ignorant*, if they can only write *jingling* verses and talk of *iambics*, admire the King's *Idyls*, and play *introits*, your *illustrious impostor* must have an *imperious* claim upon you. Forgive this *irony*, and, if you are *inclined* to be *irritable*, remember that your *infatuation* appears to me as *inexplicable* as my *indignation* may appear to you. Farewell. Yours ever, C. D.

I send you *Isaac Jefferson's inaugural* address, and his remarks upon the right *interpretation* of Scripture. He has been chosen president of the Young Men's *Institute;* and is pleased, notwithstanding the *insignificancy* of the position.

LETTER XVIII.

FROM A. B. TO C. D.

ROME, April, 1865.

My dear Friend, — What an *inflammable* and *incomprehensible jumble* was your last letter! If my new friend was *immoral*, *irreverent*, and *irreclaimable*, you could not use stronger *invectives*. Your anger is *incommensurable* with the cause; indeed, it is *inexpressibly infantile.* Your warnings are *inapplicable.* It is true that Mr. Harrison's secrets are *impenetrable,* but I see nothing about him *indicative* of *intrigue* or *imposture.* I am not so *incorrigibly idiotic* as to trust him with matters of *importance,* or to allow myself to be *implicated* in his affairs. I have no *inducement* to do so; but I am *indebted* to him for *increasing* my pleasure, and *introducing* me to many *intelligent* persons. The *inaccuracy* and *inconsistency* of your statements, I own. surprise me; and, though I do not *impugn* your kind *intentions,* I feel that what you say is *inappropriate.*

Why should you give way to this *inordinate inquietude,* and strive to *inoculate* me with the same? You would *instil* doubt into my mind, and *instigate* me to make *impertinent* and *indiscreet interrogatories.* I have an *innate, intuitive* conviction, that my friend is *irascible* and *implacable,* and would *interrupt,* and even strive to *intimidate* me, the *instant* I began to *interrogate* him; for curiosity is, in his eyes, an *inexpiable* offence. I have seen many *instances* in which he has *intentionally,* though *jocosely,* rendered himself un*intelligible* to an *interlocutor* whose conversation has bordered upon *insolence.* Though he is generally *innoxious* and *impassive,* and is *inured* to silence, and has been even accused of *insensibility,* yet he is *impatient* of *inquisitorial* questions; and the *intonations* of his voice show *instantaneously* when he discovers any wish of *intruding* into his private affairs. I, therefore, cannot so *intrude,* feeling sure that the *intrusion* would be considered an *imperti-nence*, and be un*justifiable.* You must allow me to repeat, that your *judgment* is formed upon an *inade-quate* knowledge, being based upon a few *insulated* and *isolated* facts ; and that you lay yourself open to the *imputation* of *indiscretion*, by *implications* which, when brought before a *jury*, might, if the *jurors* were *impartial*, be punished with *imprisonment.*

Pray do not put a wrong *interpretation* on my words. I own that I am *imperatively* called upon not to place myself in *jeopardy ;* but I see no reason for *inferring* that, because my friend's past life is *inscrutable*, therefore his actions have been *illegal.* Such an *inference* would surely be an *infringement* of the charity *inculcated* by the Bible. It would be an *impeachment* of my friend's honor, and a breach of the *indefeasible* right of every man, — that of keeping his own secrets.

This argument is, I think, *irrefragable*, *irrespective* of the fact, that to act otherwise would be to me *in-supportable* and *insufferable*, and to him most *inju-rious.* A mere *inkling* of *insignificant* facts is often, in these days, converted into an *irresistible* proof of guilt ; and a man of *irreproachable* and *irreprehen-sible* life may have his person and property rendered *insecure*, by the way in which the *inviolability* of his private affairs is disregarded by a foreign *judi-cature.*

An *incidental* remark, an *ironical jest*, may be deemed *indications* of principles irreconcilable with the Government. *Judicial inquisitions* and *investi-*

gations may be *instituted ;* facts most *irrelevant* to the point at *issue* may be brought forward to *justify* the proceeding ; and the *innocent individual* may be *instantly incarcerated* and *irremediably injured,* if not *irretrievably* and *irrevocably* ruined.

In our own *island,* indeed throughout all the British *Isles, integrity* is such an *integral* part of the system of *jurisprudence,* and the *influential journals interpose* such an *insuperable* barrier to the *injustice* consequent upon the *insufficiency, instability,* and *infirmity, incidental* to all men, even those who are *installed* in a *judge's* seat, that it is difficult for the *imagination* of even an *Irishman* to picture the *inadequacy* of the courts of law, the *incentives* offered to crime, and the *iniquitous impediments* sometimes placed in the way of *justice* in other countries. I could give many *illustrations illustrative* of this, but they are *incommunicable* in a letter : they would, however, *include* evidence collected *indiscriminately.*

At first, I was *inclined* to repel *indignantly* your *implied* distrust ; but although I do not choose to be *interdicted* a friendship which *irradiates* my lonely life, as the *Iris* brightens the clouds, yet I have no *implicit* faith in the *impeccability* of my new acquaintance. I see, *indeed,* the *impracticability* and *impossibility* of discovering the truth of his *improbable* and *incomprehensible* history ; but I know that he dislikes *innovations,* and will always submit to the *inhibitions* of Government. You must therefore *importune* me no more ; for you will find me *inflexible.*

We have had *inclement* weather, for the time of the year, and *icicles* have been seen at the fountains. This *inclemency* has, I am told, caused an *infinity* of *inflammatory illnesses*, *including intermittent* and *infectious* fevers, *jaundice*, and *inflamation* of the lungs. The latter, I had *imagined*, was an *inheritance* of evil *incident* only to England. The doctors use *ipecacuanha* and *jalap* freely. For my own cough I prefer *jujubes*.

The *inconvenience* and *incommodiousness* of the houses for the poor must *increase* their sufferings. They are not *impervious* to weather, and many are in *imminent* risk of falling down; but these hovels are an *inheritance* which the Romans have *inherited* from their forefathers. If an *impetus* could be given to the *inert* Government by the *imperial* power of France, there might be some *improvement*. The Romans are not so much *inactive* and *inanimate* as *inept*. Their *inanition* and *incompetency* are really not the result of their own *impotency*.

I am learning *Italian*, but as yet I am only *jabbering inaudible*, *inarticulate* sounds. It is not *irksome*. My *instructor* has written some remarks upon *indeclinable* nouns, and the *inflections* of *intransitive* verbs, which have somewhat *illumined* my mind; but I am *ineffably* and *intensely* dull in studying the *intricacies* of a new language. They appear *intolerable* and *insurmountable*. I am *involuntarily inattentive*; and this *inattention* brings forth *indignant interjections* from my *infuriated* teacher.

I assert that the *idioms* of one language are *in-*

transmutable into another; and in this position I *intrench* myself, as in an *impregnable* fortress. But he, with great *intrepidity*, attacks me, and *inundates* me with *inexhaustible*, but *inapplicable* examples of *idiomatic* expressions in *Italian* and English, which he declares to have *identically* the same meaning. As I am only just *initiated* into the language, I am *immersed* in it; but I do not work as *immoderately* as my sister, who, *independently* of her lessons, is *insatiable* and *indefatigable* in her pursuit of knowledge. She *impairs* her health, by taking a grammar with her on her little *journeys* and *jaunts*, and reading it in the *interregnum* of the dinner.

We have found the *joints indigestible;* but as some *indemnification* for this, we have an *illimitable* quantity of *ice*. *Jellies* and *jams* are also good, and our fare is upon the whole *innocuous*, though I sometimes long to make an *incision* in a *jargonelle* pear. I have before me a *jasper* vase filled with *jasmine* and *jonquilles*. My sister is the *inheritress* of her mother's tastes, and a love of flowers, which is *inherent* in her, and indeed *ingrafted* into her nature, has been *infused* into me, if such a thing can be *infusible*.

We *intend* this afternoon to visit the *identical image* of Pompey, at the foot of which Cæsar fell on the *Ides* of March. There is scarcely any doubt of its *identity*, and it will be most *interesting* to me, for it is a kind of historical *idol*. I shall look at it with almost *idolatrous* respect. It was *inhumed*, or one might almost say *interred*, for many years, and it is to this fact that it owed its *immunity* from *injury ;* for, although the *Iconoclasts,* who destroyed the *imagery* in churches, had no power in Rome, there have been many since whose *implements* would have been used against it without mercy.   I trust it may never again require *incrustation,* to make it *indestructible ;* but, even if it should be so, no *invader* can destroy the *inextinguishable* fame of those whom it recalls, and who are *immortalized* in history,——the only *immortality* which they sought.

When I have been at Rome a little longer, I shall be prepared to write an *itinerary.*   To-night there is to be an *illumination* of St. Peter's.   The *immensity* of the space occupied by the building, even without *including* the *intercolumniations* of the colonnade, will make it a splendid sight.   I should *joyfully* walk to the Piazza, as carriages are *interdicted* from passing through several streets, but my sister fears the *jostling* crowd.   As she is *invalided,* I yield to her ; besides, I am her *junior* by a year, and even in our childish *janglings* she always *imposed* her will upon me, though it often *jarred* upon my boyish pride. This is speaking *jocularly,* of course.

The *jewels* in the *jewellers'* shops, and the lovely *intaglios,* are a constant temptation.   If prudence had not been *instilled* into me, I should be ruined. Life can be spent *jollily* in Rome, if sight-seeing is taken by *instalments.*   You would be *invigorated* if you were here, and how *jubilant* should I be !   It would be a season of *jubilee* to us both.   How many churches we would visit ! but you would dislike the smell of the *incense*. If I should prove a bad *journalist*, my sister will fill up the *interstices*, and will add *interlineations* and *interpolations* to my letter. I was going to write *interpellation*, when I remembered that the word meant a summons, and would therefore sound odd. My sister and I are *individually* different; but, nevertheless, our *ideas* are *interchangeable*. You know how *indisposed* to exertion I am when the *inky* fluid is before me.

You find *internally* from your own feelings enough to say; but *introspection* is to me very difficult, though my affection is *inextinguishable*, and I could *immolate* myself at the altar of friendship. Do not therefore be *incensed* against me.

As you dislike an *itinerant* life, I suppose you are now *immovable*, for you have had no holiday since *January*.

Do your little ones play as we used to do at being *janizaries*, or do they have *jousts* with mock *javelins*? Do they ever call themselves *jockeys*, or pretend to be *jugglers* practising *jugglery*? Above all, do they make *imaginary journeys* to *Japan* across the *Isthmus* of Suez? Can you not now recollect how we sat on the *jetty*, opposite the *inn*, built at the *intersection* of the road, and how we read about *jackals* and the *ichneumon*; and how puzzled I was with the words *integument*, *indiscernible*, *indiscerptible*, *incorporeal*, and *infrangible*, and the meaning of *impetration*? Those were days when I thought that a marriage being *invalid* or *invalidated*, meant that the parties concerned were *invalids* or *ill*.

Your brother *Isidore* never dreamt then of *immuring* himself in the country, and of being *inducted* into a living, and learning to declaim about the *impropriation* of tithes; and *Jeremy* little thought he should be *induced* to do such an *idiotic* thing as marry an *Indian* woman for her *ingots*. Cannot your *imagination* recall us, with flannel *jerseys* and brown *jerkins* eating *juicy* oranges, and *indigestible* *juniper*-berries with *immense* delight; and playing with that *ironmonger's* son, who was so fond of *inveighing* against the *immorality* and *ignorance* of the world; and who, though he talked of the *impenitence* and *irreligious* conduct of his brother, used *imprecatory* words himself?

How he *inveigled* us into arguments about the right of *investiture*, and tried to explain the *intercalary* days! And how often our words were in *inverse* proportion to our sense! An *impalpable* barrier separates us from those *joyous* days, whilst the future is an *insoluble* mystery, hidden as by a *jet* black veil, but at no *juncture* of my life have I felt more contented.

My sister begs you will have an *inventory* made of the *items* in her room, and please let the *jambs* of the door be looked to. A *Jew* has been found dead here, and his wife is suspected of *infanticide;* but they do not hold *inquests* in such cases. This reminds me, — does your clergyman preach about *Judaism* and *Judaising* Christians as he used to do? I wish you could see the *ilexes* about Rome, which seem *indigenous;* also the *jagged* outlines of the

grand though not *inaccessible* mountains.   An *influx*,
I may even say an *inundation*, of visitors, whom I
regard as *interlopers*, compels me to say farewell.
Yours, &c.,   A. B.

P.S.   Have you heard that *James Jones* is going
to undertake the *irrigation* of what we used to call
the *impassable* meadow, as a *jobbing* speculation?
Do not send me another angry letter, for I am not
impassible.   I am not *inimical* to Dr. *Jackson*, but
his translation of the *Iliad* is *intolerable*.   Who *in-
stigated* him to attempt it?   I see he only puts his
initials in the titlepage.   Let me have an *invoice* of
the contents of any box you may send : I hope it will
not be *intercepted*.   I should like to see the account
of the *installation* and Mr. *Jervois's* speech on civil
and spiritual *jurisdiction*, though I have an *inveterate*,
invincible dislike to the man, and *intuitively* shrink
from him.

LETTER XIX.

FROM C. D. TO A. B.

MARGATE, April, 1865.

My dear Friend,—I *know* you will be kind
enough to accept these few lines.   I should write
more, but I have to search into a question of *kinship*
for one of my *kinsfolk*.   About the time when the
kingdoms of Scotland and England were united by
King James, a *knight*, who was somewhat of a *knave*,
and had a *knack* of getting rid of his *kindred, killed*
his wife with a *knife*, whilst he was *kneeling* on one

knee, and pretending to *kiss* her. He was hung, and his estates went to the next of *kin.* But it is said that he had a child, who was *kidnapped,* as he was playing with *knuckle*-bones on a *knoll,* by a woman wearing a *kirtle,* and a man with a *kilt* carrying a *knapsack.* A *kitchen*-maid, who *knows* only how to *knead* dough and make *kickshaws,* calls herself now the nearest *kinswoman ;* and, if she really is so, the present owner of the estate cannot *keep* it, but must *knock* under. The story will require *keen* inquiry and there will be many *knotty* points needing much *knowledge* of law to discuss. My *kinsman kicks* against the idea; but he *knows* nothing as yet of the evidence. He lives chiefly in Scotland : a great deal of *kelp* is made on his estate. His chief pleasure is in his dog-*kennel* and his *kine ;* and he leads a life as solitary as that of a *kingfisher,* and always wears *knickerbockers.* It will be the *knell* of his happiness when I tell him what is in store. I saw the kitchen-maid yesterday. She had a *kettle* in her hand, and was going to boil *kidney*-beans. I think myself that the *key* to the affair is the spite of a man who unkindly built a brick-*kiln* near my *kinsman's* home, *knowing* it would annoy him, and was obliged to take it down. He is engaged to marry the kitchen-maid, and I suspect he has *knit* together a number of wild tales. The woman is as silly as a *kitten,* and only fit to blanch the *kernels* of almonds, or gather *king*-cups for children. I doubt if she even knows how many barrels go to a *kilderkin,* or could tell the price of *kerseymere.* Good-by, my dear friend. Yours ever,

C. D.

My little pupil Gertrude has just spelt *keel*, of a
ship, like *Kiel*, a town in Holstein.   You will understand her difficulty.   As soon as she can spell the
word *kaleidescope*, I am going to give her one of
those amusing playthings, which has just been given
to me.   She does not care for *knick-knacks*, so this
comes just in the *nick* of time.   When she is very
dull, I threaten, in fun, to use the *knout*, — a word
the meaning of which she as little understands as
she does the original language of the *Koran*.

LETTER XX.

FROM C. D. TO A. B.

MARGATE, April, 1865.

My dear Friend, — The *lengthening* of daylight
limits my *leisure* for *letter*-writing, which, as you
know, was always very *limited*.   Every day we *loiter*
later on the shore.   It has a *likeness* to the *Littoral*
at Venice.   The *loveliness* of the *lingering light leads*
us to forget the *lateness* of the hour.   *Latterly*, also,
I have been *listless*, and given way to *lassitude*, and,
as you know, I *loathe* writing, and am always *loath* to
leave the *locality* where the children are.   I have
taken my *little Latin library* to the beach with me,
and *learnedly* studied *logic*, whilst *listening* to their
laughter and *laughing* voices, and watching the *lading*
of the vessels, which are often heavily *laden* with
coals.   I wonder how they can carry such *loads*.

Yesterday, however, we had a *ludicrous* adventure.
A *lively lodger*, who *lives* in our *lodging*, and is a

friend of the *landlord* of the house, *lured* me to a distance by telling me of a *lovely landscape*. I *left* my *Lexicon*, the children their *limpets*, and we set out after *luncheon*. The *loquacity* of my *loquacious* companion, and the *liveliness* of the children, made me overlook the *lowering* clouds, until a *lambent* flash of *lightning*, which *lightened* up the *lurid* sky, made me fear *lest* a storm should be at hand. I should have taken the *lead*, and *led* the way back, but I was as dull as *lead*, and *lazily* followed my companion down a *lane leading* to a church, but which wound in and out *like* a *labyrinth*.

As we stood under the *lich*-gate, my friend, who has very *latitudinarian* views, said something which I thought *libellous*, and did not *list* to hear, about the *Liturgy* and *Litany* of the English Church. He has no knowledge of *literature*, and no *literary* tastes; and his *Latinity* is *less* than nothing. His *levity* made me *lecture* him. I *launched* forth in strong *language*, and *lost* my temper; and, in my *laudable* zeal, forgot that the clouds were *looming* in the *loaming*, as the Scotch say. A *loutish lackey* in a *livery* coat came up, as I was *laying* down the *law* about the *legendary* tales of saints. "The young *lady* is *lying* in the ditch, sir," he said, in a *lisping* voice. "I don't tell a *lie*: I saw her *lie* there, and the *little* gentleman is *laying leaves* over her." The *lad*, who is in the service of *Lady Lawson*, and is much thought of by her *ladyship*, had certainly given a most *lugubrious* picture, not *lessened* by his *lachrymose* tone. My friend *leaned* and *lolled* against the *loose* gate, as though to *lose* time was of no consequence. " Near the *lower* pond, sir," said the boy ; and without *losing* a moment I ran off. My friend followed *leisurely :* a *level lawn* was on the other side of the *lane,* and the boy, *loosing* a hurdle, let me cross it. My *limbs* shook, and I stumbled and *lamed* myself, so that I *limped* slowly, though *luckily* the pain was *lulled* by fright ; but I had hurt the *ligaments* of the *left* foot.

I called *loudly* to the children, and, after the *lapse* of some moments, a *languid* voice answered from the further side of a *laurel*-hedge. It was *literally* not an instant before I was through the hedge, whilst my *lethargic* friend was a *league* behind. A sound of *lamentation* drew me, as by a *loadstone,* to the ditch. There, at full *length,* lay Gertrude, her frock *littered* over with leaves. whilst George was repeating, in a *lamentable* tone, the *lyrical legend* of " The Children in the Wood."

How *long* Gertrude had *lain* there I did not ask, but my dismay must have been *legible* on my *lineaments,* and the child *leaped* up, *put* her hand in mine, and said, " I was to *lie* there first, and he was to *lay* himself down afterwards." — " You *little lunatic,*" I exclaimed, " what will the *laundress* say ? You shall wear *linsey*-woolsey instead of *linen.* Look at the wet *loam* you have about you." — " He put dried leaves on me," said Gertrude, " and he would have *liked lavender* and *lilies ;* and he asked a *laborer's* wife who, he thought, was *leasing* in the fields, where it was *likely* he could get some, and an old woman who was *looking* out of a *lattice* gave us some *lettuce* leaves."

To keep from *laughing* was impossible. George saw my *look*, and felt they were to be *leniently* treated. " Gertrude *looped* up her frock," he said, " and it only wants *lukewarm* water, and a *lather* of soap from the *laundry*." — " In spite of my *lenity*, and the *laxity* of my rule," I replied, " you had neither *leave* nor *license* to lie down in a ditch. You are human beings, not *lambs*, *lizards*, or *leverets*, *leopards*, or *lionesses ;* neither are you *leviathans* or *lobsters*, who can dwell in the sea. You have to *live* in houses, not in *leafy* woods, and you have to gain your *livelihood* by some *lucrative* and *laudable* means. You, George, may be a *lawyer*, a *lieutenant*, a *librarian*, a *logician*, a *lexicographer*, a *lithographer*, or even a *legislator*. What will be said, if it is known that you *lie* down in ditches ? "

George *looked* at me in horror, and I went on. " If there had been even a *limpid* and *lucid liquid* in the ditch, it might have been excusable ; but *liquefied* mud, like *laudanum*, or some thick *liquor*, is too dirty, not only for a *lavatory*, but even for a *lazar*-house or *lazzaretto*." If I had called George a *liar*, his face could not have been more *livid :* he looked *loathingly* at his dress and his *leather* boots.

I wished for a *limner* to *limn* his expressive face. I am no *linguist :* my *language* was *limited ;* and, not *liking* to frighten him more, I *left* the *locality* of the ditch, and led the children across the *lea*. As we had no *luggage*, we needed no *locomotives* but our own *legs ;* to which I would, indeed, always as *lieve* trust.   Poor George evidently felt he had *lost* all chance of a *lieutenancy,* or of commanding a foreign *legion,* or being a member of the *legislature.*   He had received a *lesson,* the severity of which was only *lessened,* when, in the evening, my friend showed to him and Gertrude some tricks of *legerdemain,* and a magic *lantern,* played to them on the *lute,* and *liberally* gave them *lard* cake, *lozenges, licorice,* and *luscious lemonade.*   In *lieu* of this, I should have *liked* a *loaf* of bread, or even a *loin* of veal without *loaves ;* for, as the result of his *liberality,* George is suffering from *languor.*   Though *lithe* in appearance, he has a *liver* complaint which makes him *lethargic,* and he is often *languishing,* so I have sent for a *leech ;* meaning not the *loathsome* creature, but a doctor, who, though he is not *lawfully* and *legitimately* so called, has an excellent *laboratory,* and has made some *lasting* cures, one especially of a *limbersome* young *lass* from one of the Scotch *lochs,* whose arm had been *lacerated* by a nail stuck in the *lintel* of a door.   My friend seldom uses the *lancet,* and is expert in *ligatures :* he is fond of *lubricous liniments,* but is careful that they should be *labelled* and *lettered.*   He has a curious practice of keeping the *lees* of his medicines in bottles like the Roman *lachrymatories.*

It is said that he is a *lineal* descendant of some German *Landgrave ;* but though he behaves *loftily,* he is very *laconic* when inquires are made on the subject.

His fault is *love* of *litigation*, which makes him a *litigious litigant*, and he always has a *law*-suit on hand. He is at *loggerheads* now with one of his father's *legatees*, who disputes the *legality* of some *legacy*. I have given myself such *latitude* in my *lucubrations*, that I have only space to add, that, although you think yourself *lynx*-eyed as to the *links* which bind your new friend to you, I still doubt the *longevity* of your friendship. You are a *loyalist* in principle, and though you often talk *loosely*, you are *loyally* devoted to your *liege* sovereign; whilst he is, I suspect, a *leveller*. If you have no *leaning* to these views, your *longanimity* must be put to the test, unless, by reasoning *logically*, you give him no *loophole* for escape from your conclusions. I suspect he will some day ask you for a *loan;* these *lone* individuals are generally poor.

Have you seen a *lampoon* and a caricature, comparing a distinguished *luminary* of the age to King *Lear?* The *leanness* of the poor king, who is *like* a *lath*, is absurd: he has just *landed* from a *leaky lugger*. By him stands a Welshman, eating *leeks*, *lentils*, and *lampreys*, with such a *leer* on his face! Behind them is a knight with his *lance* in rest. Some say he is meant for a pope's *legate*. Is it true that the *lotteries* in Italy are *lavishly* used to *liquidate* the debts of the Government? Gambling seems to me a disease like *leprosy;* and the poor persons who indulge in it seem no better than *lepers*. If you go to Naples, tell me about the *liquefaction* of the blood of S. Januarius; also whether you hear much of the brigands, — those *liers*-in-wait for *lucre*, who are *levying* tribute there, which can scarcely be called petty *larceny*. I have no news, for *locally* there is none : but I *luxuriate* in this quietness. I have bought a carpenter's *lathe*, and am using it upon a *ligneous* material, nearly as hard as *lignum* vitæ.

I am told that the *lessee* of the *Lyceum* at *Loughborough* has taken a new *lease* of the building. My cousin was at the *levée* the other day, and his wife went to the drawing-room, and wore *lace lappets*, and curtsied *lowlily*. There were no *largesses* given to the servants. Mr. *Lawrence* is the new member for *Lincolnshire* or *Leicestershire*, I am not sure which ; and his uncle is standing for *Lancashire*. I hear he thinks his new home as grand as the church of S. John *Lateran*. It has a centre, and two *lateral* projections, called wings. Though a complete *landlubber*, he has a boat on the *lake*, and always talks about *larboard* and starboard. Boating is his only pleasure besides playing on a kind of *lyre*.

The *lapsing* to the bishop of the *large living* of *Lutterworth* is much talked of, both by clergy and *laity ;* but I do not think that *laymen* know much about it. It is said that it will be given to a man of obscure *lineage*, the son of a *lapidary*. He has written on the *laver* of baptism, and also on the Book of *Leviticus*, and the *Levitical laws*. *Lately*, he has been in the *Levant ;* and when I *last* met him, he told me that *leaven* was commonly used there, and that Nebuchadnezzar's disease was called *lycanthropy*.

A brother of his has published remarks upon *latitude* and *longitude*, and an essay on *logarithms;* of which he knows as much as George does of the *lustrations* of the ancients, or of the use of the *lever.* Gertrude asked me to-day whether *linch*-pin had any thing to do with *lynch* law. The irregular plurals of words perplex her much; *lamina* and *laminæ* for instance. She has finished a picture of a greyhound in a *leash,* which she thinks as good as one of *Landseer's,* only it wants a *labial* inscription that you may know what it means. Is not the *Laureate's* poem first rate?

Now, farewell : I must go and help Gertrude sow *lupins* and *larkspurs.* Your ever,   c. d.

Tell me if you see any *locusts* in Italy; and pray are *lapwings* and *linnets* common there? I should be very glad to have a good specimen of *lapis lazuli.* My sister says you will find amongst her treasures a *lacquered ladle* and a small *lantern,* both of which she values; also a very pretty box for *lucifer* matches.

LETTER XXI.

FROM A. B. TO C. D.

Rome, April, 1865.

My dear Friend, — After a *meagre meal* of *meat,* with *mawkish macaroons,* and a *modicum* of *marmalade* and *melon, meditation might* well be *maintained;* but the *mail* waits, and you will bestow your *merciless* anger upon me if I do not tell you of my *memorable* doings on *Maundy* Thursday, when the

11

melodious, mellifluous, and *melancholy modulations* of the " *Miserere* " were *marvellously* sung at the Sistine Chapel.

It would, however, have been *meeter* not to have *mingled* with the *multitudinous* and *motley* crowd who *mustered* on the *magnificent* staircase of the Vatican. The *moody musketeers,* who *moved* not a *muscle* of their faces, had but little power over the *mutinous murmurers. Mitred* bishops and *morose monks* might have *muttered maledictions* in vain, as, in one *moveable mass,* the crowd made its way up the staircase.

After *many minutes* I discovered amongst the *multifarious male* faces with *mustachios,* my *moody* fellow-lodger, the *moiety* of his features *mysteriously muffled.* The *military,* many of them Swiss *mountaineers,* with their *martial mien,* and *martinet manners, manifestly* and *unmistakably meant* to *marshal* us *mechanically ;* but the *majority* of the crowd did not choose to be *meddled* with, and some *malapert malcontents malignantly, maliciously,* and *malevolently* abused the guards without *measure :* whilst they, being on their *mettle,* tried to gain the *mastery* by *manual* force, which the mob endeavored to avoid by *manœuvres. My* brain was *mazy,* and I *mentally* resolved that a *million* of Spanish *moidores* should not tempt me again to risk such a *misadventure* and *misfortune.* In the *meantime,* the *massive* doors of the chapel were open, and after a *miserable* struggle *amidst* the *maddened* crowd, I found myself not *materially maimed* or *mutilated,* listening to the *mournful* and *matchless melody.*

I seemed to have been *miraculously* preserved. To be left without *molestation* was like the rest of the *Millennium* ; but, though I had been told that the ceremonies were *majestic*, I *merely* gave myself up to the *mollifying* influences of the *metrical* chant. I may have *magnified* the un*manageableness* of the *mighty mob* ; but I know that I had a *momentary* dread of some *monstrous mishap*, and required some *morbific medicine* from a *medical man*, before I could *manage* to sleep after the day's trial.

A lady whom I know, lost in the crowd a bracelet with a *miniature*, a *minever* boa, and various articles of *millinery* ; but this is but a small part of the *measureless mischief* done.

To-day I am going with the *Marquis* of R——, to see a private *museum*, containing some beautiful *marquetry*, *marbles*, and *mosaics*, and a *malachite mantle*-piece ; also a collection of *minerals*, *medallions* and *medals*. They belong to the *Minister* of Finance who has *married* one of my cousins. Besides being a *mineralogist*, he is a collector of *mezzotinto* engravings, and he has also some curious *monograms*, and *miscellaneous manuscripts* with *marginal* notes. I shall make *memoranda* in my *memorandum* book, but they will be *merely* as to the *meaning* of *misspelt* words. The *munificence* of the *Marquis* is well known, but I wish I had a *millionth* part of his wealth. My servant, who, though without *malice* or *malignancy*, is in the *majority* of cases quite wrong, tells me I have ten *minutes* to spare ; but I must not trust him. So adieu. Yours, A. B.

P.S. — Do you know that *Mark Maurice* has died from something having injured the *membrane* of the throat, which in some way caused a difficulty in *manducation.*

XXII.

MARGATE, April, 1865.

My dear Friend, — My *manifold* good intentions this *morning* have been interrupted. One *man* came with a *macaw* and a *marmot ;* another with *mushrooms ;* a third with *mackerel* and *mullet ;* a fourth, who called himself a *machinist*, brought a *model* of a new *machine*, the *machinery* of which has been approved by Her *Majesty.* The children then began playing with a *magpie ;* and, when I was writing a paper on animal *magnetism* for a *magazine*, some *minstrels* in the street took to singing *madrigals*, and songs of Spanish *muleteers.* There seemed a *machination* against me, especially when little Gertrude, who has a taste for *mimicry*, threw a *mohair mantle* over her, and appeared before me like a *masquerader.*

I am *magnanimous*, and can forgive them all, but my *magnanimity* has been greatly tried. I have now given the children my *microscope*, and the *minute mechanism* which they discover from it astonish them like *miracles.* Their *mirth* and *merriment* are delightful, and prevent me from being *morbid ;* but my pleasure in the children is *modified* by constant fear of the *measles.*

Sometime I will tell you a *marvelous, mystical* story I lately heard about the *mutilating* of the statue of *Minerva* in the *Munich* Gallery. We have here in the *museum*, a *mummy* injured by *muriatic* acid.

The buzzing of the *mosquitoes*, the peculiar *murmuring* and *moaning* of the wind, and the chirping of *myriads* of crickets, evince the approach of night. So good-bye. Yours,   C. D.

LETTER XXIII.

FROM A. B. TO C. D.

PORTLAND, July, 1865.

My dear Friend, — *Nathaniel* has just returned from the *Notch:* his *numerous narrations* are very *naïve;* and, *notwithstanding* his *near*-sighted and *narrow*-mindedness, he has made quite a *number* of friends. He was dressed in a full suit of *nankeen*, with buttons of a *nacreous* lustre. *Never* was a person more properly *nick-named* a *Nabob*. My *nephew Noah* the *naturalist* is *negotiating* with his *neighbor* for a treatise on *neutralizing* fluids. He has been trying to make me understand the properties of *naphthaline.*

The other day I *nabbed* little *Noe* in the act of *nicking* the *nostrils* of the *new* marble *Nylghau*, which stands in the *niche* under the picture of a *Numidian* crossing the *Nore.* In my anger, I called the little fellow a *Norwegian*, and gave him such a knock as *numbed* him. His *nurse*, who believes in *necroman-*

cy, *noyau*, and *nostrums*, ran for some *nux vomica ;* but a *nectarine* which I took from my *nuncheon*-basket rendered her aid completely *nugatory.* Now, my dear, do not *nudge* me too hard in your *next* letter. I *need* no one to tell me that my conduct is *nefarious ;* my temper *notorious ;* my action *novercal ;* my example *noxious* to *novices ;* and, in short, that I am a *nuisance* in the species *Novus-Homo.* Be assured that, in future, *nought* shall prevent my using my best endeavors to make myself the *nucleus* of this happy family.

I think I have already *notified* you of my belief in the *Norns*, and *notions* about *naturalization.*

Nehemiah is a *notary* public, and is *never* unoccupied, except when suffering from *nystagmus* or *nictation* of the eyes.   Yours ever,   A. B.

LETTER XXIV.

FROM C. D. TO A. B.

BATH, June, 1865.

My dear Friend, — We were at table, enjoying our *natch* of beef with *nastursion* salad, *neat's-foot* jelly, and *nutmeg* melon, when my *namesake*, in handing me your letter, threw down that beautiful marble *Naiad*, breaking the *nautilus nearest* to it, at which *Nehemiah*, the waiter, laughed heartily. I am *naturally nervous*, and given to *nugacity*, as you have often told me; and, in the excitement of the moment, I behaved as *naughtily* towards him, as I found, on reading your letter, you had done towards little Noe :

so you see that it is not *necessary* for me to take *note* of your *naughtiness.*

Dr. *Nickerson* says, "*Nature never neglects* to warn us in regard to our *nourishment.*" *Nancy* — who, by the way, is no *neophyte* — is suffering from *neuralgia* and *nausea,* owing to the *niggardly* regimen of which she *now-a-days* makes use. I think she will be obliged to have recourse to *narcotics.* I have received several *nice nick-nacks* from persons in this *neighborhood;* for example, a box of *Neapolitan* figures, a *neat* knitting-sheath, a pretty mazarine-blue silk *needle-case,* — the giver called it "*nazareen-blue,*" — and a *Nymph* of *nacre* holding a *noggin* which serves for a match-box.

It is reported that Mr. *Nailor's* family are in such *necessitous* circumstances that he has been obliged to sell his valuable *nautical* library. I see by yesterday's *newspaper,* that he refuses to acknowledge that his *nephew* is a *non-conformist.* How much better it would have been for his family if he had been *neutral* in politics.

Our young people enjoy the chemical lectures prodigiously, particularly the experiments with *naptha, noctiluca, nitrogen,* and *nitric acid.* It was *noticeable* that the youthful lecturer was somewhat *nonplussed* by questions put to him by Miss *Newman,* a silly *namby-pamby,* who insisted that *nap, neat, nail, nervous,* have each but one meaning. Mrs. *Newbury* asked her, for sport, where she had been *nurtured.* She answered, that she had made her *novitiate* in a *nunnery,* from which she had come out to prepare for her own *nuptials,* and that she was about to marry a *numismatic.* As Mrs. Newbury was not familiar with the term, she thought Miss Newman was a *neologist.*

Nestor has a *night-hawk* in a cage made of *Nicaragua-wood.* It makes a singular whizzing *noise,* quite disagreeable to me. I wish it were a *nightingale* instead. Yours as ever, C. D.

LETTER XXV.

FROM A. B. TO C. D.

ONEIDA, July, 1865.

My dear Friend, — Do you know that Mrs. *Oglethrope* is both *officious* and *obtrusive,* besides her *oddity.* It is laughable to hear her tell of *obtenebrations, oafish* figures, and *oasis* resembling *oasts;* of an *odorous obcordate* pulse like *okra,* and of being in a state of *obdormition,* which almost produced an *offuscation* of her *optics.* She says that she writes *obituaries* for the *opulent,* and studies *ophthalmoscopy* most *obdurately* in *order* to prevent *obesity,* to which she is inclined; but I *opine* that she is too *opiniative* to *obtain* what she calls an *opiparous* living by her writings.

Owing to the *opportuneness* of Mr. *Owen's* obliging *order,* it will be *optional* with *Obediah* to bring his *optograph* or not.

Would you believe that he allowed himself to be *oppressed* by Mr. *Oldham's opprobrious* remarks? I do wish that Mr. Oldham would *oust* his *oraculous opinions,* and *oblige* himself to *observe* that *order* necessary for those who wish to be called *optimists,* or become *oracles* as *orators.*

Olivia asked me if you were studying *ornithology, orismology,* or *oryctography:* to which I answered, that I had *observed* you make mistakes in *orthoepy* and *orthography,* and, although you write *oscitantly,* you are as *orthodox* as an *octogenarian;* and I saw no *ostensible* reason to suppose that you would not *occupy* your time in what is *ordinarily* considered as most useful.

Dr. *Osgood* is much troubled with *otalgia.* I am told that he is an *oneirocritic,* as well as an *onomatologist.* The *only* fault I find with him is, that he is too *opinionative* and *one-sided,* and too apt to *oppugn* every one : he says the honors he receives are *onerous* to him.

I showed him the ring you sent me, and he says, it is not *opalescent* enough for an *opal,* and is nothing more than *opalized* wood : he even tried to make me acknowledge that it was *opaque.*

I *ought* to tell you that I have succeeded to the *ownership* of my aunt's *olograph.* Write soon, and believe me yours, affectionately, A. B.

LETTER XXVI.

FROM C. D. TO A. B.

PORTSMOUTH, August, 1865.

My dear Friend, — Do you remember hearing of a singular *occurence* which took place in the *old-*

fashioned octagonal house, corner of *Ochre* and *Ocean* Streets, some twenty odd years ago ? A similar one, which has just *occurred*, will, I think, never be *obliterated* from my memory. An *official*, perceiving an *offensive odor* while passing near the *outer* porch of said house, burst *open* the door. In a room *opposite* the *opening* lay a terrier in the first stages of decomposition, and the attenuated dead body of an aged female, *outstretched* upon a pallet of straw. On examination, her lower limbs were found to be *ossified*. Around her, and within her reach, were bits of bread, bones, and *offal*. No *occular* demonstration was necessary to prove that they had been brought there by the dog. There was no food in the closet, nothing except a small *osier*-basket in which were a few *onion* tops, and some bottles containing an *oleaginous* substance *offensive* to the *olfactories*.

To think that this woman, *once* noted for *opulence* and pride, and whose *ostentation* and *opprobriousness* brought *odium* upon her, should die an *outcast*, with none to care for and nourish her in her *old* age but a dog ! May *omniscient* God forgive her *oppressors !* I shall take the first *opportunity* to send you a copy of some verses *obituarily* inscribed to the dog. It is my *opinion*, that our newly *ordained* minister will take the *ordering* of the funeral, as he *ordinarily* does not *object* to render such services.

I am so *oppressed* and *over-weary*, that I fear I shall be *over-tedious*. We have been *overwhelmed* with company this summer.

Did you not tell me that your *odd* friend, Mrs. *Olcott*, made you *octennial* visits ?

Our children were *over-anxious* to see the *orang-outang.* They say he eats *olives, oranges, orgeates,* and *oat-cakes.*

He is very *obdurate,* and it is difficult to force him into *obedience.* He evidently has great *objection* to making his *obeisance,* and is quite *outrageous* when his keeper tries to make him put on *overalls.* Adieu for this time,   C. D.

LETTER XXVII.

FROM A. B. TO C. D.

PETERBOROUGH, July, 1865.

My dear Friend, — I have been *permitted* to enjoy the *pleasures* and *pastimes* of a *picnic,* in *part* at least, without its *pains* and *penalties.* We had just left the steamer *Poughkeepsie,* in which we sailed to *Philadelphia* to make some *purchases,* when we *perceived* that the draw of *Percival* Bridge was open. *Providentially* we *procured* shelter, from the *perpendicular* rays of the sun, under a *projecting* roof.

Presently we saw a crowd of children rushing towards the bridge. They were all *plentifully* supplied with *provender,* which they carried in *panniers, packages,* and *pinafores.* Not being able to *pass,* the boys *pushed* and *pulled* each other in a most *pugnacious* manner, until a *pedantic personage* drove them all, like a flock of *pigeons,* upon a narrow *peninsula.* The girls amused themselves with making boquets of *pennyroyal* and *pentadactyls,* and the boys in catching *polliwogs,* and *pulling* and *pounding* every thing upon which they *placed* their hands. A *phalanx* of them *persisted* in *playing* with some *putrescent* fish, which occasioned such a *pestiferous* odor, as caused me to fear the renewal of my *pharyngeal* trouble : however, having a *phial* of homœpathic *pills* in my *pelisse*, and a *pharmacologist* at my side, I sat *placidly* waiting the result. A *pettifogger* said, that, in all *probability*, we should form a sort of *phalansterianism*, at least for the day ; so the *puerile* portion of the *party* attacked their provender most *persistently*. *Pears, peaches, pomegranates, pineapples, plums, puddings, pies, pastry, pound-cake,* et cætera, caused some *prevarications* and disputes among hungry brothers and their sisters, who had been *previously* cautioned by their *parents* to beware of the *prevalent* custom of children, of eating up their *provisions* all at once.

A *philanthropic, patriarchal* woman *proposed* to some of the *poorer* children, — as a *palliative*, I supposed, for their small *proportion* of edibles, — that they should play school ; but a gentleman, who appeared to be *patrolling* the party, *pronounced* her *proposal preposterous.* In lieu, thereof, he ordered one of the boys to *procure* a *peck* of roasted *pea-nuts*, and *parched* corn, for which he *paid* from his own *pocket.* You should have heard the little *plebians* shout their thanks, as he *poured* it out in their midst. I must confess that I was very much *prejudiced* in his favor, notwithstanding all his *provincialisms.*

In the midst of the *prevailing* hilarity, the draw unexpectedly closed, and a car, *propelled* by four *powerful* horses, appeared : there was a general stampede, so that in a few minutes we were left in quiet *possession* of the *premises.*

The *proprietor* of our *protective* asylum *proffered* us some pulse ; and, as I am not very *punctilious,* I was easily *prevailed* upon to accept of his *politeness.*

Do you notice that I am *prone* to make mistakes in my *punctuation?*

How much *patience* is required to do things *properly.* Ever yours, A. B.

LETTER XXVIII.

FROM C. D. TO A. B.

PORTSMOUTH, Aug., 1865.

My dear Friend, —— What a *queer* child you are, to talk of experiencing pleasure in company with *querulous* children, near a *quagmire!* Really, you are the *quintessence* of *quixotism.* I think you must have felt a little *queachy* and *quesy* when you *questioned* that *quack.*

This morning a *quarrier* brought me a piece of rose-*quartz* of a *quadrangular* form, and *quite* as large as a *queening.* He says, that the whole *quarry* back of our house is *quartziferous.*

Last evening we played in *quartette,* producing quite a sensation in the neighborhood. They say that the *queen*-dowager, who was riding by, ordered her postilion to stop ; and that she *quietly* listened for more than half an hour in a most *quiescent* state. Is not that *quite* complimentary?

Quintilius brought me a *querquedule*. I hardly know what *quality* of food it requires: I put it with the *quails*, and noticed that it ate up a *quartern* of barley in a few moments.

When *Quintius* receives his *quarterage*, he means to *quit* his present studies, and *qualify* himself for the law. He begs you to give yourself no *qualms* on his account, as he is in no *quandary* as to the propriety of such an avocation.

I am told that his interests have *quadrupled*; therefore there need be no trouble about the *quantum* to meet expenses.

You know that I am not *querimonious*; yet, I could with difficulty refrain from *quarrelling* with Quintius's mother when she *queried* about giving him a *quarto* volume of the history of *Quebec*, and actually went to a second-hand bookstore in search of a copy. By the by, Quintius is now *quirister* of the *Quaker* Church.

Our *quince-trees* are all dead. My flower-beds are filled with *quitch*-grass: the seeds of *quaking*-grass which you sent me did not grow; please save more for another season. Truly yours,   c. d.

LETTER XXIX.

FROM A. B. TO C. D.

ROWE'S POINT, September, 1865.

My dear Friend, — Your *racy* letter, in which you *reproach* me of not *reminding* you to *reclaim* the *residuary* payments belonging to your brother *Ra*-

phael, is *received,* and my *reply* is, that I hear that the law which secured it was *rescinded.*

Uncle *Richard* has just *returned* from a visit to Boston, where he was much gratified with the *reception* of our troops : he says, " The *regulars returning* from *Richmond* were *reviewed* in the *rear* of the *Revere* House. They looked *remarkably* well in their new *royal* blue uniforms, and *received* the most *roaring* applause for their perfect evolutions. They *resumed* their march, and *reached* their camp to *repose* from their fatigues." These men *richly* deserve the *reward* which a grateful nation *renders* them for their gallantry in their defence of a *righteous* cause.

Roxana Richardson has been here ; she *really* looked charming, with her *ruby* lips and *rosy* cheeks : she was dressed in a *red riding-hood,* made of *ratteen* instead of *ratinet.* Poor child ! she was terribly frightened, having been in the midst of a *rabble* of *ragamuffins, roughs,* and *rowdies,* who were *running* after a *rhinoceros* which had escaped from a menagerie. The proprietor, fearing that their *reiterated* shouts would prevent the *recapture* of the animal, *repeatedly remonstrated* with them, and finally offered a *reward,* which proved more efficacious than all his *reasoning.* After *raising* such a *riot,* the *refractory* creature took *refuge* in a *refreshment* saloon, and was *recaptured* by means of a *reconciliatory* meal, which he devoured with great *rapacity.* I will not *recapitulate* the articles of food he is said to have eaten, for it is not *rational* that a *rhinoceros* should *relish roast* beef, *raw* mutton, *rumpsteak,* ra-

gout, *rennet*-custard, *radishes*, *raspberry*-tarts, *rhubarb*-pie, and *raisins*, equally well : however, the proprietor of the *refectory required* a large *remuneration*, for which he was justly *rebuked*. The matter was left to *referees*, who, with a *realizing* sense of justice, made a *rebatement* or a *reduction referable* to the state of the case.

I intend to make you the *recipient* of a valuable *recipe*, and I hope that you will soon feel yourself *recuperating*, and acknowledge its *re-invigorating* qualities. Do not *return* the same *resolute refusal* to all my *remedies* for your *rheumatism*. I cannot *relinquish* the hope that, by a *repetition* of the *repellents*, you will be entirely *relieved* from all *rheumy* affections.

I have nothing to *remark respecting* the *reasonableness* of *Rosaline's* conduct. Let her go into *rhapsodies* over what she will, it is useless for her *relations* to endeavor to *restrain* her ; opposition will only *renew* open *rebellion*.

I am sorry to *relate* a misdemeanor of your *reputed* well-behaved Rover ; with no *reasonable* provocation, no *respect* for my feelings, and no *regard* to consequences, he *ruthlessly* killed the charming *ring-ousel* you sent me, for which he was *retributed* in a manner' he did not seem to relish. I *relinquish* all hopes of *retribution* for the pains I have taken in *repeatedly reproving* him for his *recklessness :* he remains refractory, and is only *restrained* by a *rueful* glance at the *rod*.

It is *rumored* that you intend to visit us. I hope it is true.   Yours as ever,   A. B.

LETTER XXX.

FROM C. D. TO A. B.

RIVERSIDE, August, 1865.

My dear Friend, — Your letters are received like the *refreshing rain ;* but you should *remember* that I do not attempt to *rival* you in the *roguery* with which they are *replete.*

Who should I *run* against last Wednesday but *Ruggles,* who has come here to *rusticate.* You never saw a person so altered ; he is *round-shouldered, raw-boned,* and *robustious ;* his *red* hair has become *rough* and *ragged,* and his cheeks, though *rubicund,* are not *ruddy ;* his gait is *rocking* and *rickety.* His visits are becoming *regular,* and he makes us *roar* with laughter by *repeating* quaint *riddles, running* after little *Ruth round* the *rhododendrons,* and in the way he *rides* out on *Roan* the *racker.* This morning he set out to *ride round* the town : just as he *reached* the *railroad,* the *report* of a gun frightened his horse, which *ran* down *Rainbow* Street as far as the *Rappahannock rolling*-mill, where he was thrown into the *receptacle* for pulverized *rosin : raising* himself, he seized the *reins,* and *remounted* the *rearing* animal, and *returned, regardless* of a *rupture* which will cause *rigidity* of the muscles of his *right* hand, if not timely cared for.

His appearance was so *ridiculous* as to excite the children's *risibles ;* and though it was natural that they should laugh, he could not *realize it,* and re-

quired that I should punish them *rigorously*, instead
of *requesting* them to go and play at *rolly-pooly*, as I
did.

We are having the house new-*roofed*, and putting
in a new range with the view of making it more
roomy.   One of the workmen found a *rook roosting*
in the *rotunda*.

We go through the *rustic routine* of *reaping* our
rice and *rye*, mowing our *rowen*, and gathering our
russets, rhubarb, red-peppers, radishes, rue, and *rushes*,
and digging our *ruta-baga* and other *roots ;* as your
father says, to save *rupees*, but, *rather*, as I think, to
afford us that *rural recreation* which *requires* con-
tinual exercise in the open air.   He is always *rational* in his *requirements :* he is *revered, reverenced,*
and *respected* for his *republicanism, righteousness,* and
religious tolerance.

Relief made such a *rumpus* about her *ruff,* or *ruf-
fle,* that I *rummaged* your old *round*-box till I found
the *rumpled rag* of a thing.

Uncle Reymonds sent us some fine *rowan-trees,*
raspberry bushes, and *ranunculus* roots : I am in *rap-
tures* with them.

Keep me in your *remembrance.*   Adieu,   C. D.

LETTER XXXI.

FROM A. B. TO C. D.

SYRACUSE, September, 1865.

My dear Friend, — How *singular* it is that *some*
people *seem* to require *such* large *sums* of money !

We have just been reading of a *Scotchman*, named *Stewart*, whose *services* to William the *Stadtholder* secured for him a *salary* of *several* thousand *sequins*, which ought to have *sufficed* for his living in a *style* suitable for one who had never before *swerved* from customary *simplicity*, yet his *sovereign saw* fit to allow him a *sinecure*.

Also, a *singular story* of a *sycophant*, who *succeeded* in getting introduced to the *sagacious* Pope *Sextus Sixth*. Once this Pope gave him a *string* of beads, with this *salutary* advice, uttered with *seeming* simplicity, " *Strangers* are *scarcely safe* travelling in these *States*; the *safest* way for you is to *start* before *sunrise*, take a *siesta* at noon, and *secure* a conveyance for home at night." He must have *set* out alone, for he tells of his *sufferings, sitting* in a *solitary* place for *several* hours, and afterwards *seeing* no one but *savage*-looking *soldiers*. He was *seized* by a *sentinel*, who demanded to see the Pope's *signature*. In his anger he called the *soldiery* a *set* of *squalid, stolid, sluggish, stupid, self-sufficient stipendiaries*.

And of King James, who *set* out on the *sixteenth* of *September* for a *splendid* tour; at *Southampton* he touched for *scrofula;* thence he went to *Somersetshire*, in company with the high-*sheriff*. At *Southgate* he was received with *such* signs of joy that he *supposed* all discontent excited by his measures had *subsided;* but the *sagacious* gentlemen of *Shropshire* said, that their manner of treating their *sovereign* was no test of their *subsequent* acts; they well knew that *suavity* of manners and modified *submission* were not always *satisfactory* to a *seer* who could *see* no farther than the *See* of Rome.

Have you heard of the Swedish *sculptress* who writes Latin *stanzas,* which she sets to music, and *sings* with style and *spirit* to all *strangers* who visit her?   She has also composed a *symphony :* she lives in a *simple,* and, as far as is *suitable* to her *station,* in a *somewhat secluded* manner.   It is *secretly* said that she *sympathizes* with the *Swedenborgians.*

But why should I *squander* my *slight* historical knowledge upon you, who *spurned* to read the *sprightly* tales I sent you, and accused me of *squandering* my time in reading *spurious* traditions.

I acknowledge that I feel *somewhat squeamish* in *sending* you this letter ; methinks you will look *squintingly* at it.   As ever, yours,   A. B.

LETTER XXXII.

FROM C. D. TO A. B.

SQUANTUM, September, 1865.

My dear Friend, — Could you see us *sitting* on the old *settee,* in this most *sequestered* and *salubrious* spot, *satiating* ourselves with *savory* meats, *sandwiches, sausages, stews, sauerkraut, scalloped* oysters, *sturgeon, swordfish, sprats, salmon, souse, squash-pie, strawberry-cream, sherbet,* and *surrounded* by *scullions* and *saucepans,* you might think your *sanitary* advice was not only not *serviceable* but quite *superfluous ;* yet I am sure you would *sanction* the *steps* we have taken in *secluding* ourselves from *secular* affairs (I *speak* of *secularity* only in regard to business concerns), and be as *sanguine* as ourselves as to its *salutary* results.

Cousin *Stephen* fell from a *scaffolding*, and severely injured his *shoulder*-blade; and, though he is also suffering from *sciatica*, yet he *studies Sanscrit*, and writes very *satirically*. He is really *scribatious;* and his *songs sparkle* with *sarcasms* and *satire*, against which relationship is no *safeguard*.

Last Saturday, *Steven saturated* the hair of my *Scotch* terrier with *salad*-oil, and then *submerged* him, head first, in a brook which runs on the *south side* of the house. I came in *season* to be the little creature's *savior*. When I took him from the *sturdy* boy, who was *striving* to keep him *still* by holding his nostrils so as to *stifle* him, the animal had nearly ceased *struggling;* just then, *Susie shouted, "Stop!* we are coming;" and *six* or *seven* children *screamed simultaneously,* "We are coming to *see* Jack baptized." I was about to *scold* Steven, when he informed me in the most *serious, sanctimonious,* and *sanctiloquent* manner, that baptism was necessary for the *salvation* of poor Jack, who had *stolen* a *staunch* piece of *steak,* for which the cook threatened to *scourge* him *severely.* As you may well *suppose,* my anger was immediately *subdued,* and I *sympathized* with the dear child in his childish *simplicity* and *sympathy* for the *sinner* Jack; and, the more so, when I *subsequently* recollected how hard I had *striven* to avoid answering his *seemingly sceptical* questions last *Sunday,* about Rev.

Mr. *Saunders' sermon* on the *salvability* of the *souls* of men through baptism.

This morning, *some* one threw a *squib* into a broken *square* in my *sewing*-room, which burst, *setting* fire to *some skeins* of *stocking* yarn : my *sister*-in-law *smothered* it, and, *singular* to *say,* we cannot discover whence the squib came.

The *sketches* in the *semi*-weekly Gazette are *scandalous ;* I have no patience to read them : however, I found a few *scraps* which may *serve* you, thus : —

" At one time the *Sicilians* were *supplied* with *sal-ammoniac sufficient* for their apothecary *stores* from the eruption of Mount Etna."

" *Sulphuret* of antimony was used in *staining* the eyebrows of the ladies of *Scutari* and *Salonica :* they paid for it in *shekels* of *silver ;* the value of a shekel was fifty cents."

I must *stop,* as *Susanna* is *searching* the house for me.   Affectionately yours,   C. D.

LETTER XXXIII.
FROM A. B. TO C. D.

TORONTO, October, 1865.

My dear Friend, — I am *tarrying* with Mrs. *Taylor,* formerly Miss *Towne,* a *teacher.* She *tells* me that *travelling* in stage-coaches in *Tennessee* is very *tedious.* She *tried teaching* in a planter's family ; but as he was *tyrannical,* and she would not be *trifled* with, or *tyrannized* over, she removed to a *tavern,* where she gave private lessons in *trigonometry* and *taxidermy*, until Mr. Taylor, a *tallow*-chandler from *Tarrytown*, brought her here. Though she is quite a *technologist*, and very *thoroughly* acquainted with the English language, in which she is always *terse*, yet she is at *times* almost *taciturn*.

Last *Tuesday* I was witness to a *terrible tumult* in nature. Some *thought* it was the *termination* of all *things terraqueous*. In *turning* round the *tannery*, with *Tristan*, we saw the church *tower torn* off and *twirling* through the air. *Thousands* of *tadpoles* and small fish were *thrown* on *terra-firma*; the *telegraphic* poles were upraised in many places. All in a *twinkle*, so to say, the *thunder* roared, the rain fell in *torrents*, the wind blew tempestuously: I *think* it must have been a *tornado*.

I have joined the *teetotalers*, though I am still a *tea-drinker*. I have commenced *taking* lessons on the *tambourine*. *Thaddeus* is *teasing* me to buy a *tan-terrier* for him. Mr. *Twing* offered him one *thirteen* months old, answering to the name of *Tray*; a charming little *thing*, which has learned many *tricks*.

How are matters *thriving* with you? Have you *taken* the *thrashing*-machine? Who is the best *thrasher* among the boys? Is *Tabitha* as much of a *termigant* as ever? I wish you could see the *tortoise* and *turtle*-doves we have here: they are beautiful. Please send us the *Traveller*, *Tribune*, and *Transcript*; also, some work on *Transcendentalism*. I am *transcribing* "*Titcomb's Transubstantiation*," and when I have finished it, I will *trouble* you to read it over; also, the copy of "*Talbot's Transfiguration*," which I forgot to leave with you.

Every thing in my room is *turned topsy-turvy* since I have been writing: the children have *tied* the chairs *together*, and are *trying* to ride *tandem*. Every now and *then they touch* Tray to *teaze* him, and make him *twinge*. Poor fellow! he has much *tribulation* with the little *tyros*. We *think* of *tendering* our *thanks* to the poet *Tennyson* for the *truthfulness* of his *touching* descriptions. Our gentlemen spend much time in *theological* discussions; two of them have studied *theology*; indeed, *Thomas* is *thought* to be a good *theologian*. The children puzzle *themselves* trying to find out the meaning of the *terms* which they frequently hear; for example, *theocracy*, *theodicy*, *theologaster*, *theomachy*, *theopneustic*. I must acknowledge that I am not so thoroughly versed as to be able to satisfy the *talkativeness* of *three turbulent* boys.   In haste, yours,   A. B.

LETTER XXXIV.

FROM C. D. TO A. B.

TEWKESBURY, October, 1865.

My dear Friend, — What a *tendency* some *tolerant* people have to *take* the *truncheon* of command. So you *threaten* me with what you have *transcribed!* *Tendering* you my sincere *thanks*, permit me to tell you that I prefer my own *tranquillity* to the *tediousness* of reading *transmundane transactions;* besides, I am just now *tormented* with the fear of being left without a servant. Our *trustworthy Tabitha* has just made her *triennial threat* of leaving us; and *this time*, it is, alas, *too true!* She is to be married to Mr. *Thompson, tobacconist*, and sets out on her wedding *tour* next *Thursday*. You have always accused her of *termagancy ;* but I assure you she will make a *treasure* of a wife for a good-*tempered* man, and be *truly* a helpmate in his business, for she understands *trading* and *trafficking*. She has received a great many useful presents; a *tea*-set, *tidies, trays*, tinware, *table*-linen, etc.; and what pleases her more than all is a *trumpet* for her husband, who belongs to a *troop* of *trumpeters*. Just now she seems to have a *tulipomania*, and is collecting bulbs from every quarter to plant in the garden of her new *tenement*. Mother gave her some *tuberose* bulbs, *trumpet*-honeysuckle, and *thyme* roots. *To-morrow* I shall *transmit* my *testimonial* of *tenderness*, in the form of a *towering* wedding-cake and *thimble*-berry wine.

We were sitting at table to-day, when mother asked a gentleman if he would take *turkey, turbot, turbit*, or *tripe*, to which he answered. by asking if we had any " *trilobite ;* " mother replied, we have some " *trilobates* " in the green-house, and " trilobites " in our museum. This *trivial* remark introduced several interesting *topics* of conversation, in which Mr. *Twichel, treasurer* of the *Typographical* Society, and *trustee* of the *Thompsonian* Institution, *took* a *timely* and spirited part. I assure you that he is not only a *talented* man, but quite a historian : he *talked* with the same ease of *translocations* and *transitions* as of *traditions* and the *Talmud*, of *tarentulas* and *tardigrades* as of men and their *times*. From him I learned that *Tamerlane tarnished* his name by acts of *treachery* and cruelty *towards* the *'timorous Tartar tribes,* who *trembled* before him.

When Mr. Twichel and I conversed *tête-à-tête,* I found that he was very *tenacious* of his *Teutonic* origin, rather given to *testiness,* and quite *theatrical* in his manners.   He has promised to pass *Thanksgiving* with us, and to bring me some *terns'* eggs, a work on *tertiary* formations, and a *text*-book on *thaumaturgy.*

There is much talk in *town* about the last *testament* of *Thurlow,* the *tragedian.*   Several persons are ready to *testify* that they can produce *testimonials touching* the validity of their claims as relatives to the deceased.   It is astonishing how much *tenderness* a pile of dollars calls forth !

Do not be *terror-struck* at my cruelty, when I *tell* you that I have *tethered* your terrier to a *tree.*   As ever,   Yours affectionately,   c. d.

P.S. — I should *trespass* longer on your time, had I not the *tic-doloreux.*

LETTER XXXV.

FROM A. B. TO C. D.

UTICA, October, 1865.

My dear Friend, — I can *understand* why you feel so anxious about being left without help, — you *undertake* too much, and you *undervalue* your own ability.   I have been *uninterruptedly* occupied with *uninteresting* people all day. *Usually* I rise at six, but this morning I was *undisturbed*, and slept long enough to *use up* my time and *upset* my plans. When I entered the breakfast-room I found *Ulalie*, with *uncombed* hair and *unwashed* face, *usurping* my right to the head of the table; by the by, she is a *useful* little body, and was doing her *utmost* to *unfold* the wrinkles on grandpa's brow. You can imagine how *ungraciously* he received my excuses for an *undue* amount of sleep. I often wish he was not quite so *uncomplimentary*, and so *unconscionably* strict in some petty matters. Before we had half finished breakfast, the *unruly* little *urchin*, *Uriah*, ushered the *ubiquitous* Mr. *Underwood unceremoniously* into our presence. *Unfortunately*, I have the *uttermost* disregard for him; and there I was obliged, on grandpa's account, to sit and listen to his *unintelligible* twaddle *upon utilitarianism* and *utopianism*, for nearly two hours.

Undoubtedly you have heard that *uncle's ultimate* intention is to make an *ultramontane* expedition as soon as his *ulcerated* limb is healed.

Yesterday we were *unexpectedly* called upon by persons with whom we are entirely *unacquainted*, to give our *unbiased* opinion respecting the *umbrageousness* of certain trees which they had selected for the town. We did so in the most *unselfish* manner, being *unactuated* by any secondary motive; but it appeared that my remarks in regard to the *unhealthfulness* of too much shade were *unacceptable*, for one of them coolly informed me, without even an attempt at *urbanity*, that he thought I must be *unaccustomed* to thinking profoundly, at which I took *umbrage*; but deeming it *unadvisable* to give myself any *uneasiness* about the matter, I told them that grandpa would act as *umpire*, and left the room.

I send you some *unadulterated* rose-water, which I bought of an *uncouth*, *unsightly* Indian woman. She seems to have an *unconquerable* hatred to the whites: they say her temper is so *uncontrollable*, that she strikes any one who offends her; strange to say, I am not in the least afraid of her; she has always treated me with *undeviating* kindness. Poor woman! her situation is *unenviable*.

Did I tell that cousin *Uriah* had no sooner left the *University* than he was appointed *usher* to our high school? The people are very well satisfied; and he promises to be a *useful* acquisition.

Many thanks for the little painting in *umber* you sent me: it is much admired.

Do not *upbraid* me for my short letters: I assure you that you are *uppermost* in my mind, and I should write oftener if I were not continually *urged* to go out.   Affectionately,   A. B.

LETTER XXXVI.

FROM C. D. TO A. B.

TEWKSBURY, November, 1865.

My dear Friend, — I have been *vascillating* between writing to or *visiting* you; and, after *various* pros and cons, I *verily* believe I will write, though

I am *vexed* to find myself so *void* of thought. If there were such a thing as a *vacuum* in nature, I should think I had it in my brain; for my mind, if not entirely *vacant*, is *vaporous* and *vapid*, and I fear my letter will savor of *vapidity*. My poor *Varus* is sick, so that I cannot play the *voltigeur* any longer. There is great *variableness* of opinion among the *veterinarians* who have him in charge: one treats him for a *varicose vein*, and another for the *varioloid;* one will give him *vervain*-root, *vinegar*, and *vapor*-baths, and another has a famous preparation of *vitriol*, *volatile*-salts, and *vetch*-grass, which has a most *vivifying* influence. I am at *variance* with them all, and would prefer *venesection* to all their *venomous*, *vitiating*, *virulent* medicines. I am not given to *vituperation*, yet I *vehemently* exclaim against torturing the poor dumb beast.

Viola came here this morning to bring me a *variegated verbena* and some *violets* in a pot. They were *very* similar to those Mr. *Vezie* brought from Mount *Vernon*. I *value* them greatly, for they continually remind me of dear *venerated* Mrs. *Vere*, who, even in a state of *valetudinarianism*, *volunteered* to show us *where* to find *wild* ones in *Wyoming woods*.

I am told that there is a *voluminous* work in preparation *vindicating* the *villainous* conduct of Judge Jeffreys, and the right of King James to carry out his *violent*, *vindictive* measures, through the agency of such a *villain*. Will such a work tend to *vitiate* public morals? I hope the *visual* organ of the public mind is too *virtuously* clear to be blinded by the *vociferations* of a *visionary* writer, whose only merit consists in *vaunting* of James's *varnished virtues.*

Give yourself no uneasiness about V———'s *vocalizing* to strengthen her *vocal* powers : if you had heard her *vociferate*, as I did the other day, you would say that she has *voice* enough for any purpose to which she may wish to apply it. She is even more *voluble* than,   Your affectionate   C. D.

LETTER XXXVII.

FROM A. B. TO C. D.

WALTHAM, November, 1865.

My dear Friend, —— *Wednesday we went* into a factory in *Ware, where* we saw some most *woe*-begone looking *women weaving woollen waistcoats* and *wa*ter-proof *wearing* apparel of various kinds. Being wholly unacquainted *with* such kind of *work*, I found myself asking such questions as children of a smaller growth are always propounding ; as, *What* time is required to *weave* a pair of *waist*-bands? *Where* do you sell so many *woven* hose? *Which* loom is the best? Are *white woollens warmer* than colored ones? *Which* is the *warp* and which the *woof?* One *weaver* contrived to put "I *warrant*" or "I *wager*" into all his answers to my questions with *why*, which, what, *when* and where : he looked *waggishly*, and appeared to *wonder* as much at me as I did at the cog-*wheels, water*-tanks, and *wool*-combers.

We went from the factory into a *zoological* garden, where *were weasels, wolves*, a *wild boar*, a *wal*-

rus, a *whale,* some very beautiful specimens of *wrasse, winged-fish, widgeons, whimbrels,* and a *zam-bo* acting the *zany.* *Willie wishing* to feed some of the monkeys, the keeper *willingly* allowed him to bestow his *walnuts* and *waffles* upon what he called a *well*-behaved family; and he was so much delighted in *watching* their manœuvres, that he did not *wish* to go home, and I *went* away *without* him.

The *wind* is *whistling* through trees *wreathed* in *warm*-tinted robes, and *wherever* I turn I hear *whisperings* of *winter's* approach; but as I am no *winterling,* I cannot *welcome* it. Those who are *weary* and *worn* may *while* away their time in the chimney-corner, and *whistle* and *whittle* in concert with the crackling *wood* and smoking turf. I love better to sit in a *woody* grove, listening to the *woodpecker,* the *whippoorwill,* and the *whirring* of the partridge. The *whizzing* of insects, and the *whirling* of leaves, moved by a summer's tiny *whirlwind,* are my pastime. I send you a bottle of dried *whortle*-berries and a box of *wedding* cake, together with some *wheaten* bread of my own make, which I hope will be *well* received.

I have been *washing Winifred's wax* doll: it is not as good as new, but, on the *whole,* is no *worse* for the *watering.* I intend to dress her in a *whitish worsted* skirt, with a red linsey-*woolsey waist,* trimmed with black, and black *wristbands.* Now I am going into the kitchen to make a *Welsh*-rabbit, and *wish* you *would* come to partake of it as you

used to do.   Am I not *whimsical* to *write* such odd
words ?

There come the *white washers*, and I must go.

Your *well-wisher*,   A. B.

LETTER XXXVIII.

FROM C. D. TO A. B.

WILBRAHAM, December, 1865.

My dear Friend, —— Notwithstanding all our *wor-
rying* about the *wickedness* of the man who tried to
wrest our homestead from us, under the pretence
that it would increase our *wealth* and be for our *welfare* to *yield* to his *wishes*, here we are, in good old
Worcester Street, *waiting* for you and other *youthful*
members of the family to celebrate this *year's wide-
awake* with uncommon *zest*.

I have just been standing at the *window, watching*
a *youth, yonder*, under the *yew-tree*, who is *wonder-
fully* clever in *whittling wedges* for *windows*.   I am
so *well* pleased with some I bought *yesterday*, that I
will call him in to whittle some more, for it already
feels very *wintry ;* one would almost think the *wain-
scoting* was *wholly* out of repair, for the *wind whis-
tles* in somewhere, and the old green *Wilton* carpet
heaves like ocean's *waves*.   Were it not for the
warmth of the furnace, the thermometer in this room
would be down to *zero*.

I must tell you of our success in collecting curiosities for grandma's museum, who says we must have
had a *witch*-rod to find them, and also of our *where-*

abouts since your last meeting us. On our way home from our *wandering* tour to the *White* Mountains, we crossed the *Winnipiseogee* on the steamer *Wachusett, winding* our way between several small islets. When we landed, we *wound* our way through an alley of *willows*, where we found a *wounded yak*, belonging to a gentleman of *Wolfsboro'*. His *wailful* moans sounded like the *wailing* of a person, and excited our sympathies so much, that each *wanted* to do something for his relief. I attempted to help free his crooked horns, which were entangled in a withered bush; though he was apparently *weak* from loss of blood, yet he *writhed*, and *winched*, and *wrenched* so, that he sprained my *wrists*, and I was obliged to desist. I found a bit of his horn which I took along with me; then we brought home a miniature *yawl*, made of birch bark and some *wampum;* then a friend gave us teeth of a *xiphias*, and a *zebu's* hoof, so that, as you see, grandma's store has much increased.

We saw a *zibet:* I could scarcely tell the difference between it and a *young* fox.

Grandpa's *zeal* for playing *whist* has *waxed* greatly, and he makes a *yoke*-mate of *whomsoever* he can persuade to *while* away the evening with him. I *willingly* play now and then, but every evening I cannot, — it *wastes* too much time.

Winter has really set in, and it is *welcome* to me on account of having an opportunity to read and study. Apropos of reading, whilst I was looking for copy of *Xenophon's* Works, I found the biography of *Ziskah*, the blind Hussite *warrior*, who *wrought*

18

such an influence on his people, as the story goes, that after his death they made a drum of his skin to inspire his men and make his enemies tremble. I found also a *Zendavesta* ascribed to *Zoroaster,* and am *watching* for an opportunity to *withdraw* to my chamber to run them over, for there is no peace in trying to look into a book where little children are *whirling* and *whizzing* and *writhing* and *whining* and *whisking* and *wringing* and *whipping* about like *wild*-fire.

Do not call me a *Xantippe,* because I scold about them : just at this moment, Master *Waddie,* who is often a *wrongdoer,* and a *wily* little fellow *withal,* is *yachting,* as he calls it, in my new willow *work*-basket; *whilst* a *younger* brother is trying to stuff a roasted *yam* into Xerxes' (Mr. *Woolcut's* Newfoundland dog) mouth, and *Zachariah,* with a piece of chalk as large as his hand, is *working* with all his might to make the hair-cloth sofa look like a *zebra.*

By the by, what do you wish to have done with the *xanthine* you sent home? The next thing I expect, you will send a *xyster* and a *yataghan* for the sake of variety, or to excite wonder in us *worldlings.*

The children begin to *yawn,* and the dog to *yelp,* which *warns* us that they all *want* to go to bed, to rest their *wearied* limbs.

I have a *yearning* desire to see *you* rather than *your writings,* so farewell for the present.

Yours, in love, C. D.

Cambridge : Printed by John Wilson and Son.

TESTIMONIALS.

New York, February, 1865

I have used "Otto's French Grammar" since its publication, and consider it the best book on the subject. It is based on the most modern Grammars published in Paris; it is thorough, and full of idiomatical expressions that can be found in no other work.

LUCIEN OUDIN, A.M.
Instructor of the French Language, N.Y. Free Academy.

I have used "Otto's German Grammar." I consider it a very good book; its abundant vocabularies, and its fulness in idioms, are especially useful. The appendix, also, is very valuable, containing, as it does, some of the most popular and characteristic German Poems which may be turned to many uses.

Feb. 1, 1865. ADOLPH WERNER,
Professor of German, New-York Free Academy.

Washington University, St. Louis, Jan. 2, 1865.

Mr. S. R. Urbino.

Dear Sir — It gives me great pleasure to inform you that I have introduced your edition of "Otto's German Grammar" in my classes in this University, and that I regard it as the very best German Grammar, for school purposes, that has thus far come to my notice. Your German editions of the "Immensee," "Vergissmeinnicht," and "Irrlichter," are great favorites among my pupils; and your "College Series of Modern French Plays," edited by Mr. Ferdinand Bôcher of Harvard College, I regard as very useful for the recitation room, and for private reading.

Yours very truly,

B. L. TAFEL, *Ph. D.*
Professor of Modern Languages and Comparative Philology in Washington University.

DICTATION EXERCISES. By E. M. SEWELL, author of "Amy Herbert," and by L. B. URBINO. Boston: S. R. URBINO.

"We are already deeply indebted to Miss Sewell, and this little book adds one item more to the list of valuable books which she has furnished to us and our children. This is emphatically a school-book with a soul in it, and we think nothing can exceed the skill and ingenuity with which these exercises are drawn up. No teacher can glance at it without at once perceiving its importance to him; and in our opinion, in the teaching and spelling, it has not its equal. — *Transcript.*

DICTATION EXERCISES. By E. M. SEWELL and L. B. URBINO. (pp. 174.) Boston: S. R. URBINO.

"Bad spelling is so common, in spite of all our schools, that it is worth the while even of an accomplished writer like the author of 'Amy Herbert" to prepare a good spelling-book; for such is the volume before us.

"It is arranged, however, on a plan so novel, in English, as to deserve special attention. The words are arranged in continuous, though rather comical, sentences, which are to be written down, from dictation, by the learner. The lessons are progressive, and cannot fail to interest more than the old columns of disconnected words. It is well printed by Mr. Urbino."— *Commonwealth.*

If a child of average capacity, that has been drilled in an ordinary spelling-book, and then subjected to a course of lessons in this book of Dictation Exercises, cannot spell correctly the words of the language, it would prove, what I do not believe, that correct spelling *cannot* be attained by *all* pupils, by seasonable *study* and *drill.* I believe that every public and private school in America would be greatly benefited by using this valuable treatise.

Very truly yours,

WILLIAM E. SHELDON.

Check Out More Titles From HardPress Classics Series In this collection we are offering thousands of classic and hard to find books. This series spans a vast array of subjects – so you are bound to find something of interest to enjoy reading and learning about.

Subjects:
Architecture
Art
Biography & Autobiography
Body, Mind &Spirit
Children & Young Adult
Dramas
Education
Fiction
History
Language Arts & Disciplines
Law
Literary Collections
Music
Poetry
Psychology
Science
…and many more.

Visit us at www.hardpress.net

Im TheStory
personalised classic books

"Beautiful gift.. lovely finish.
My Niece loves it, so precious!"

Helen R Brumfieldon

⭐⭐⭐⭐⭐

UNIQUE GIFT

FOR KIDS, PARTNERS
AND FRIENDS

Timeless books such as:

Kids

Alice in Wonderland · The Jungle Book · The Wonderful Wizard of Oz
Peter and Wendy · Robin Hood · The Prince and The Pauper
The Railway Children · Treasure Island · A Christmas Carol

Adults

Romeo and Juliet · Dracula

Highly
Customizable

Change
Books Title

Replace
Characters Names
with yours

Upload
Photo for
inside page

Add
Inscriptions

Visit
Im TheStory.com
and order yours today!

CPSIA information can be obtained
at www.ICGtesting.com
Printed in the USA
BVHW042319180819
556172BV00018B/2476/P